Peacefulness
BEING PEACE AND MAKING PEACE

EDITED BY DAVID CADMAN & SCHERTO GILL

Spirit of Humanity Forum

Peacefulness

BEING PEACE AND MAKING PEACE

ACKNOWLEDGEMENT

The editors would like to thank all the contributors to this
volume and the Spirit of Humanity Forum for their help
and support in publishing this book.

CONTENTS

FOREWORD

MIKE HARDY, CMG OBE

THIS BOOK WILL BE ON my desk and not my bookshelf for quite some time. There is so much that resonates in this timely collection for both scholars and practitioners grappling with approaches to peace and peaceful relations. Many of these approaches continue to fail in so many contexts and communities, but here, Scherto Gill and David Cadman bring hope to the disappointed and new lenses for our visions for changed times.

In this collection of insights, I liked the ambition of the excellent *whole* volume matched by the passion in the *individual* chapters and I liked the way it draws from work in academy and from practice in the field. Peacefulness as an idea, as a way of life and as an approach to lived reality, is carefully defined and explored and we are left in no doubt of the clarity of purpose of each contribution.

The essays combine this passion and ambition with controversy. There will be bits that inspire most of us, if not all. Equally, some may disagree with, or want to place different emphases on both the narrative and conclusions. But, no one will doubt the commitment and emotion with which it has been formed. This articulation of peacefulness and the challenges it brings to our lived reality is real spiritual leadership and as with great leadership, we are offered the opportunity to disagree alongside the energy and capacity to think through new ideas and new inspirations.

When I first met our editors, Scherto and David, their calm, confident and controlled enthusiasm for peace was entirely captivating and they bring this, undiluted, to this carefully nurtured volume. The result has refreshed my desire to see what can be mobilised by bringing very personal peacefulness alongside peace within our communities and neighbourhoods to peace in the public realm. These three dimensions, the personal, the communal and the public realm, for me, unlock an exciting appreciation of peace – for which some work so hard – and *liberate* ideas of peacefulness from violent conflict. In our troubled times, making peace our default rather than our response, and *keeping* the peace rather than finding and/or building it, seems both powerful and comforting.

At a recent Spirit of Humanity Forum in Reykjavik, where so much of this rich narrative unfolded, Scherto and David had asked me to join a panel. I had been prepared to talk about the work of my Centre at Coventry and my then current work in peace-building that had been significantly influenced by a visit to President Carter's Library in Atlanta in the US. Above the President's office door is the encouragement: *Waging Peace.* I had reflected a lot on this in the ensuing weeks and months. I have long and continuously been inspired by President Carter's recent work – his passion for freedom and democracy and his energy – interestingly in all the three dimensions of personal, community and public space. The thought of 'waging', fighting and campaigning for peace was very attractive – and probably described well what I humbly aspired to do in my work. But, for the Reykjavik Forum, Scherto and David were quite directive: "In your academic and personal life, we know *what you seek to do,* Mike," they asserted, "so we are more interested in *why you do it.*" Now there was a challenge and I took it to be a challenge for us all.

This insightful book will help us answer that important question and help us to position ourselves and our communities for peace and peacefulness. Living peacefulness is an active thing to do, not a state that we simply aspire to achieve. This notion of positioning is so much more powerful and sustaining than the campaigning or 'waging' of my past approaches. So, what must we do as professionals, as scholars and as practitioners and how must we infuse in the behaviour of others, strong reminders of our humanity and our baseline need to live in harmony in whatever complex context we find ourselves?

Our more traditional approaches to exploring transitional justice and the dynamics between this and social movements; our interest in the *movement* of people, and the displacement and diaspora that this creates, as well as our studies of representation, of inclusion and political institutions, all describe reaction to created contexts – responses and special measures to address human experience. Perhaps one area more than these others, can help us mobilise the three dimensions at the core of the book: trust. For many, trust is a critical quality in relationships, or even with oneself, and the trust between community members and between citizens and the State is critical to support confidence in our abilities to release our inner peacefulness.

What remains to be seen is whether peacebuilders can, like this enthusiastic and informed team of authors, take a stand, embrace the core message and help bring about the transformations we all seek.

Mike Hardy, CMG OBE is Professor of Intercultural Relations and Executive Director of the Centre for Trust, Peace and Social Relations at Coventry University

August 2017

INTRODUCTION

THIS BOOK EXPLORES THE STORY of Peacefulness. It is the fruit of a year-long international dialogue held in 2015-2016 that sought to understand the nature of peacefulness and how it might be cultivated and nurtured towards creating a global culture of peace. This dialogue series was sponsored and facilitated by the Guerrand-Hermès Foundation for Peace (UK/France), in partnership with the Fetzer Institute (USA) and the HÖFÐI Reykjavík Peace Centre (Iceland). It was carried out in preparation for the Spirit of Humanity Forum held in Reykjavik on 27-29 April 2017.

This dialogue series highlighted several concerns in the field. The first was that for some years, the study of peace seems most often to have been undertaken within the context of warfare and violence. In such a context, peace is perceived as the opposite to war and the end of conflict resolution. Hence peace becomes something 'out there' that can be imposed, or at least settled, upon disorder and violence.

The second and connected concern is that in most peace studies, there is an underlying assumption about human beings as fearful, self-seeking and egoistic. Thus, our moral judgements are always motivated by self-interest and our individual needs and desires. This idea of human nature regards human relations as instrumental and social institutions and governance as control mechanisms that are installed to regulate human behaviours.

Thirdly, continuously present in the field is a fundamental division between occidental and oriental conceptions of peace. Western perspectives appear to be more concerned with outer situations, such as the causes of war, and the prevention of war through political structures and economic development; whereas Eastern philosophers are more interested in exploring inner stillness, and the personal effort to free oneself from desires and temptations. Therefore, it would seem that Western approaches to peace tend to focus on external harmony, accord and respect for citizens, institutions and nations, whilst Eastern strategies are more oriented toward personal virtues and inner qualities.

To address these concerns, this book proposes that an appropriate understanding of peace cannot be limited to that which it is not. Indeed, such an understanding can only come about by appreciating and perceiving peace in and of itself, most especially through exploring peace not as something that is imposed from outside, but as a shared human aspiration, rooted in our innate peacefulness, and our relationship with others and within our communities and societies. When presenting peacefulness as connected to the state of being human, we are able to overcome the simplest division between inner and outer peace, and positive and negative peace.

For these reasons, we suggest that peace and peacefulness be explored within three domains: first, within our state of being, as an aspect of spirituality; then in our relatedness, including communal relationships and social harmony; and, thirdly, in the public realm, including socio-economic systems, political structures, and global collaborations.

Conventionally, Western peace studies are undertaken mostly at the third level, but we are convinced that it is almost impossible to tackle the issues arising in the public realm without a proper understanding of the inner and spiritual dimensions of peace, experienced and practised as a collective endeavour and a communal/relational way of being together. We argue that peace can *only* arise out of these forms, and then through the support of appropriate socio-economic systems and political structures. Even the first of these matters, inner peacefulness or a spiritual state of peace, can only be explored properly when we begin to appreciate who we truly are. For as long as we are blinded by egoistic misconceptions of ourselves and our potential, we will not be able to see peace clearly. As long as we allow the increasingly discredited, but still dominant, image of humanity as selfish, aggressive and separate to continue to shape our understanding of who we are, we will be trapped into having to see peace only in the context of violence.

As the contributors to this book illustrate, the possibility of seeing ourselves as we truly are is offered by researchers from different disciplines. Examples include the research done by the biologist, Humberto Maturana, and his colleague, Gerda Verden-Zöeller, who make it clear that we are by nature a loving species and that by nature we are communal and nurturing;[1] and the work of anthropologist, Douglas Fry, who challenges many assumptions about our natural inclination for aggression and violence and shows that we possess a strong potential to make peace by preventing, limiting, resolving, and transforming conflicts without violence.[2]

They also draw on teachings from diverse faith-based traditions which affirm that humans are fundamentally peaceful beings and suggest that divine peacefulness resides in each person, and that peace and harmony are the true fruit of integrating our inner state with all that is out there. No wonder the great teachers, such as Jesus and the Buddha, have urged us to love one another and to see that true abiding lies in loving-kindness, compassion, joy in and for others and equanimity. And despite the many years of conditioning that might have eradicated our natural inclination to care for each other, in our most intimate and private realms, we do. We care for each other and we ask to be cared for.

So the principal quest of this book is to explore how we might cultivate and extend our inclinations for, and hence need of, loving relatedness and peacefulness, first to ourselves as persons, then into our nearest communities, such as our families and the local communities in which we live and work, and then further into the wider realms of our public lives, including deepening and enriching relational processes to expand love and compassion to strangers, communities of others, and the world at large.

There is an important footnote to this story. Urgency. We now know that a certain way of being has brought us close to catastrophe. We face urgent problems of climate change, poverty, and financial instability. Equally, we are confronted with terrorism, violence, and the devastating global consequences of refugees fleeing from war, famine, and oppression. The qualities that will enable us to meet these challenges lie not in furthering those that have been the cause, but in developing and sustaining those that bring us together and help each other.

Perhaps for the first time as a species, we face questions about our survival and this makes it ever more necessary that we once again become who we truly are, *Homo sapiens-amans*, a loving and peaceful people.

Hence, the most important contribution of this book rests in its insistence on the relevance of a spiritually-rooted and ethically-oriented conception of peacefulness to global socio-economic-political structures. In other words, the book postulates that peace cannot fully be expressed as our innate state of being without it also being the basis of the structural conditions of a society in which we live in harmony together, and vice versa.

In exploring this, we pose three questions:

1. How do we understand our inner peacefulness?

2. What are the conditions that help us to extend our innate peacefulness into the communal and wider public realm?

3. What forms of economic, socio-political and institutional structures, as well as educational processes, are necessary in order to nurture peacefulness and enable a culture of peace?

This book is divided into three parts and each part sets out to address one of these questions from different, but interconnected perspectives. In this way, the chapters in the book are not treated as individual or as if they stand alone, but, instead, without losing each contributor's distinct voice, they form an integral part of one collaborative endeavour. The book, thus, demonstrates a fresh and much needed approach to inner peacefulness, inter-communal harmony and international relations.

We hope that this publication, the first for the Spirit of Humanity Press, will make a contribution to a deeper and refreshing discussion of Peacefulness and its practise in private and public life.

---

1. H Maturana Romesin and G Verden-Zöeller, Edited by Pille Bunnell, 2008, *The Origin of Humanness in the Biology of Love*, Imprint Academic.

2. D Fry, 2005, *The Human Potential for Peace: An Anthropological Challenge to Assumptions about War and Violence*, Oxford: University of Oxford Press.

PART I

PART I

BEING PEACE

INTRODUCTION

THE FIRST PART OF THE book offers a distinct way to understand peacefulness from a spiritual perspective and establishes the basis for us to further discuss how peace might be nurtured not only in our inner being, but also in our outer expression. How the two become one.

Since antiquity, the notion of peace has been understood as more than an absence of war, but that it is a state of our being, a human virtue, a disposition. This inward-looking understanding of peacefulness is regarded as part of our spiritual life and the experience of quietude, prayer, contemplation and stillness lies at its heart. At the same time, this inner serenity or spiritual depth can radiate peacefulness to others and the wider world.

From somewhat different perspectives and drawing on their rich personal experiences, our three contributors in this first part of the book make a strong case that peacefulness is what defines the fundamental way we are as human beings and that it is by *being peace* that we bring peacefulness to those around us and to the world at large.

In Chapter One, David Cadman, Harmony Professor of Practice at the University of Wales Trinity St. David and an Associate of the Guerrand-Hermès Foundation for Peace, proposes that, "peacefulness arises from within us as an expression of who we have always been and whom we may become." It arises from *being peaceful*. Referring to research into human nature in the disciplines of social psychology and biology, his Quaker upbringing and education and from the wisdom teachings of different religious and faith traditions, he further proposes Love as the essence of all that is, including the profound learning in and from silence.

This rich and provocative starting narrative is expanded in Chapter Two by Sister Maureen Goodman of the Brahma Kumaris who considers the connection between inner and outer peacefulness and whether such a division is real. She speaks of an awareness of self as soul, an awareness that requires inner silence. Equally, she suggests that our *being peace* is the foundation of the transformation we seek in the world.

In Chapter Three, writer and educator, Four Arrows, aka Professor Don Trent Jacobs, presents the indigenous perspective that peace is ultimately about harmony and interbeing within the whole. He speaks of *wolokolki-ciapi*, the ability to focus on and learn from the relationships in one's own environment in order to live in balance with all that is, and how this "serves as a guide for understanding the idea of inner peacefulness." Rather than distinguishing between opposites, such as the sacred and the profane, the religious and the secular, mind and body, human beings and Nature, the indigenous peoples view these paired 'opposites' as complimentary dualities. Based on this view, peacefulness embraces the supposed conflicts and fierceness embedded in Nature, but, without its presence, violence emerges.

This part of the book brings forward an important common thread which weaves the remaining chapters together in a coherent way. This thread is marked by courage, fearlessness and the daily practise of inner silence and stillness, all stemming from a conviction that there is something greater beyond ourselves, the transcendent. By turning towards and tuning into the transcendent, peacefulness is truly found in the realm of the spiritual.

CHAPTER ONE

BEING PEACE

DAVID CADMAN

IN WRITING THIS OPENING CHAPTER and being mindful of the argument put forward in the Introduction, my proposition is this: peacefulness arises from within us as an expression of who we always have been and of whom we may become. It is rooted in love and compassion and is nurtured by stillness and silence.

We are so used to looking for answers in the external world of things and events, placing our enquiry 'out there' and making that enquiry by what is called objective observation, that the suggestion that this might be fruitless – or even that it might not be entirely adequate – is likely to be received with derision. But suppose this derision is ill-founded. Suppose that when it comes to the quest for peacefulness, it is possible that our inner being is the best place to start – perhaps even the only place to start. For might it be possible that peacefulness is not really a thing or an event that can be found out there, but that it is a way of being that arises, can only arise, from within? Perhaps peacefulness can only be found by *being peaceful*.

My proposition is that this may be true, may always have been true; that peacefulness is and has always been, not only a possible, but a necessary way of inner being. Which is to say that we have never been, nor could we ever be, truly or most completely ourselves without inner peacefulness. We cannot be at one with ourselves and with others without *being at peace*.

As I write these words, I am aware that they will be thought to be hopelessly pious and idealistic. Not part of the 'real world'. But this may not be because the words themselves are false. Perhaps, arising in quietness, they simply won't be heard above the incessant cacophony of a dominant ideology that drowns out all others. They will not be understood because we have come to accept and live by another set of words, loud words, an ideology of acute separation and selfishness – 'more for me and me first' – not murmured, but shouted. In this brash world, inner peacefulness is regarded as no more than a private fantasy.

However, it is important to recognise that this notion of being separate and apart from the whole is particular, which is to say that it has been chosen. It is not absolute, and it is certainly not a rule of Nature. We have chosen it, even if we were unaware of doing so. Most likely, we did so because we were not aware of there being any other choice. Because we had been told that it was so, we thought there was only one 'reality' and this is it. But, of course, that is not true, there *are* others. In contrast to separation, there is wholeness, a wholeness moreover that accepts and includes differentiation. In contrast to selfishness, there is the notion of the common good, a common good moreover that accepts and includes the wellbeing of each one of us. And although such notions are today deeply counter-cultural, they are part of our most ancient history, our origins. Who we truly are is rooted in notions of belonging and community.

The point that I am trying to make, and I accept that it is no more than one point of view, is not that there was once a Golden Age, a time of undifferentiated wholeness or 'being at one with' – although many creation myths are based upon such a possibility, a garden paradise from which we have been expelled, for instance – I am proposing something else: it seems to me that there has always been a tension in the human family between our separateness and our belonging. However, the point to note is that, until quite recently, the relationship between these two, between the separate and the whole, was balanced both by way of personal experience and of social structure and order. It is perhaps over no more than 400 years or so and, most especially, during the last 50 years, that a damaging and disruptive imbalance has come about. And, of course, by encouraging separateness and by diminishing the place of relationship and community, the balance between the two has now been disturbed to such an extent that deep-rooted human qualities, such as love, compassion and peacefulness have come to be seen as being, at best, part of a private world, having nothing to do with the 'real world' realms of work and public governance.

If we are to challenge this, as I wish to do, if we are to discover ways of being that are loving, compassionate and peaceful, we need to understand how this imbalance has come about; discover and understand how it was that our ancestors who, at one time, regarded themselves as being part of the whole, began, instead, to see themselves as being separate and apart. For, albeit that its modern form is of a different kind, much more exaggerated and disordered, it seems that the beginnings of this separation are, indeed, ancient too.

WE ARE INNATELY PEACEFUL

In their book *The Origin of Humanness in the Biology of Love*, social biologist, Humberto Maturana, and his colleague, the psychologist, Gerda Verden-Zöeller, propose that our most ancient ways of being, our origins, were loving and communal, learned in families as part of an extended childhood. We were *Homo sapiens-amans* and this original quality of lovingness is so embedded in us that living in a society that denies it is not good for us. It makes us unwell. But, as Maturana and Verden-Zöeller go on to say, there came a time when these 'matristic' characteristics were overtaken by the arising of a relatively more recent patriarchal culture – overtaken, but not obliterated though.

Here is the story, or perhaps one version of the story. In the Neolithic period, somewhere between 10,000 and 5,500 years ago, we had begun to live a settled and communal agricultural life in which we lived in community, learning to cultivate the soil and husband domesticated animals. As Anne Baring and Jules Cashford say in their book, *The Myth of the Goddess*, this manner of being was accompanied over time by a communal consciousness that regarded the world as ordered and entire, the recognition of:

> An essential relationship between an invisible order, governing
> the revolving phases of the moon, and a visible earthly order,
> embodied in the cycles of human and animal life, and [...] in
> the cycle of the seasons and the agricultural year.[3]

The expression of this order with its lunar cycle was the Great Goddess, the Goddess of Vegetation and Harvest. The qualities and manifestations of the feminine and the masculine were integrated into an interconnected whole. But then this somewhat settled world was disrupted by the arrival of "nomadic tribesmen from the East."[4] This invading wave, was of the Kurgan peoples, who were later known as Indo-European, although they were neither Indian nor European. They came from the steppe lands between the Dnieper and Volga rivers of what is now Russia and the Ukraine. They led a predominantly nomadic life. They rode horses and wielded axes,[5] worshipping not the goddesses of the earth, but the gods of the sky,[6] and they imposed upon a culture that was agricultural and sedentary, egalitarian and peaceful, a culture that was stratified, pastoral, mobile and war-oriented.[7] Their social system was hierarchical and dominated by powerful males with a male priesthood.[8] Maturana and Verden-Zöeller call them *Homo sapiens-aggressans* and under their influence the:

> Cyclical lunar imagery of the goddess culture was either gradually replaced by the predominantly male deities and solar mythology of the Kurgan peoples, or fused with them in the often uneasy union that [was] transmitted to later Greek and Celtic culture.[9]

Thus, it was that a culture of union was overcome by a culture of separation. But not all cultures and societies were invaded and subdued. Not entirely. The invasion did not reach the island of Crete, where the Great Goddess continued to be experienced as, "a flowing, dynamic energy that could manifest in a swarm of bees, a dolphin's joyous leap, a flight of birds, the coiling of serpents and sea creatures as well as in the human gesture."[10] As Baring and Cashford state:

> Unlike many surrounding cultures the island of Crete was not invaded in the 1,500 years from 3000 to 1500 BC, and so it offers a unique insight into how a Neolithic society evolved without disruption into a Bronze Age one while still retaining its belief in the unity of life.[11]

If this ancient Cretan society, a society which believed in the unity of life, provides us with a glimpse of a surviving matristic culture, what does it show us? It shows us a world shaped not by patriarchal or matriarchal hierarchy and separation, but by integration and notions of transformation and regeneration, a society in which feminine and masculine energies are intertwined in a relationship of whole and part. In this continuously unfolding relationship, the male god represents discontinuity, arising and declining in an annual cycle of vegetation, whereas the goddess represents continuity,[12] the ever present.

The possibility of this, for us important, relationship between wholeness and separation was later expressed by the ancient Greeks in terms of *zoe* and *bios*:

> This essential distinction between the whole and the part was
> later formulated in the Greek language by two different Greek
> words for life, *zoe* and *bios*, as the embodiment of two dimensions
> co-existing in life. *Zoe* is eternal and infinite life; *bios* is finite
> and individual life. *Zoe* is 'infinite' being; *bios* is the living and
> dying manifestation of this eternal world in time.[13]

Bios is contained within *zoe*, as part of the whole.[14] So here, from our
ancient past, we are offered an expression of that which I want to propose:
the possibility of a wholeness, a sense of the common good, that *of necessity* includes an individual life that *of necessity* is lived as part of the whole.
A mutually reinforcing and *harmonious* relationship of part and whole.

And I add this because I believe it tells us something of interest about our
present quest for peacefulness – this Cretan society was apparently a
peaceful society. "Cretan towns," say Baring and Cashford, "were not
enclosed with defensive walls, and nowhere in their art is war or violence
celebrated."[15] Somewhere here, then, there is the suggestion that peacefulness is nurtured by particular social and cultural modes of being. There is
something about a harmonious society, a society in tune with natural cycles
of coming to be and ceasing to be, that is aligned with being at peace; and,
conversely, there is also something about societies that are divided, strongly
hierarchical, societies that accentuate separation, which suggests that they
are not inclined towards peacefulness.

This is important, for it is these very notions of separation, division and
hierarchy, especially male hierarchy, that characterise the dominant
ideology of our time and which, thereby, hinder the quest for peacefulness.

WE ARE LOVING

In writing this chapter, I have been in correspondence with two of
Humberto Maturana's colleagues, Simón Ramirez and Sebastian Gaggero,
and I have asked them whether their work also suggests an innate peacefulness in our ancient being. Having discussed this matter with their
colleagues at Matriztica in Colombia,[16] they say that it does: "Peace is

fundamental to our origin and to the way in which we have come to be who we are."[17] Reality, they say "arises from the ways in which we explain ourselves,"[18] and what we take to be peacefulness is caught up in this. To understand peacefulness, they say, we have to be aware of the extent to which our understanding is set within particular cultural contexts. And we have to explore and question these contexts.

The work of Matriztica is founded upon an understanding of our 'emotional grounding'[19] and our lineage, which they claim arises from an ancient manner of being that was loving and expressed in language founded upon intimacy and nurturing relationships:[20]

> The ancient mother-child relationship that brought us forth is one in which love was conserved. If this giving and nurturing of love had not been present, we would not have survived, because the systemic relations of the niche of our being, the organism niche set within an ecological unity,[21] would have triggered a disintegrative interaction in our being.[22]

The experience of love, they say, remains very important to us because, by our nature, we want to be present with others:

> Despite all the explanations of our world that reduce our expectations of each other, the experience of love remains very important to us because, by our very nature, we want to be present with others. Without love, we human beings cannot become free of our fears and prejudices. Without love, we do not know how to conserve or talk about what really happens to us.[23]

> So, instead of thinking about peacefulness within a cultural dynamic that sees it only as a kind of behavior that occurs between periodic episodes of war, we need to see it as being conserved within our innate emotional configuration, our innate manner of being.[24]

In 2008, Humberto Maturana and Ximena Dávila proposed the 'Psychic eras of humanity' as a way to understand and explain the different eras of our conserved being arising from our earliest cultural origins.[25] In this, they proposed six eras, each one of them founded upon the fundamental emotional configurations of their time, rooted in everyday behaviours of coexistence. Each was described in terms of its basic or fundamental emotional dynamic:

1. Archaic psychic era: love as a spontaneous happening.

2. Matristic psychic era: love as desired coexistence.

3. Appropriation psychic era: the appropriation of truth and submission to authority.

4. Modern psychic era: the dominance of authority and alienation in power.

5. Postmodern psychic era: confidence in knowledge that one knows what one thinks one knows, with the temptation of omnipotence, arrogance and blindness in knowing that we know what is said to be known.

6. Post-postmodern psychic era: a great opportunity arising out of reflection and conscious ethical action.

And it is in the shift from the early inclusive and whole culture of the matristic era to the later cultures of appropriation, dominance and alienation that our innate loving and peaceful manner of being has been overcome, albeit not entirely overwhelmed.

BEING PEACE

These stories from our ancient past suggest that what we believe in, what we take to be true, matters. They also suggest that the characteristics and qualities of our personal and social relationships matter as well. After all, as the Buddha taught in the opening stanzas of the *Dhammapada*, "with our thoughts we make the world." The outer arises from the inner.

I am a Quaker. I was born into a Quaker family during a time of war in England. My early life, up until the age of 18, was shaped almost entirely by the Quaker mode of being as I went to a Quaker co-educational boarding school. Quakers are well-known for their peace testimony. It matters to them and, for this, in the past, they have been punished or at least marginalised. Because of his conscientious objection to war, my own father was taken to court, accused of sedition. So, I was nurtured in peacefulness. It was set within me.

Quaker testimony is particular. It has a discipline. Inclined to 'see that of God in everyone', Quakers are disinclined to violence in both their personal and public lives. They take the second commandment seriously: "That ye love one another." I sometimes wonder what part of this commandment is not understood by those who profess to be Christian, but justify war. After all, the commandment is not, "That ye love one another if you can, but if you can't that ye kill one another." Nor is it, "That ye love those who love you, but kill those who want to kill you." It is: "That ye love one another." And as if to make it even more clear, Jesus taught: "You have heard that it was said, 'Love your neighbour and hate your enemy.' But I tell you love your enemies and pray for those who persecute you."[26]

And this is not only about war. The Quaker testimony takes the practice of peacefulness into the detail of our everyday lives. Here is William Penn in 1693:

> A good end cannot sanctify evil means; nor must we ever do evil, that good may come of it [...] We are too ready to retaliate, rather than forgive, or gain love and information. And yet we could hurt no man that we believe loves us. Let us then try what Love will do: for if men did once see we love them, we should soon find they would not harm us. Force may subdue, but Love gains: and he that forgives first, wins the laurel.[27]

"Let us then try what love will do." This testimony arises not from a high-minded idea, but from personal practise, and so Quakers are urged in their Advices and Queries to search out whatever in their own way of life may contain even the seeds of war,[28] and then pay attention to them. And because my focus is not war and violence, but peacefulness, in and of itself, I want to turn that Advice around and propose that we seek out and nurture the seeds of peacefulness – seeds which, it would seem, must germinate in the darkness of our inner being – and pay attention to them. I want to know how we might seek out such seeds of peacefulness and nurture them.

And then, of course, there are the teachings of the Buddha, which are rooted in compassion and peacefulness and based upon the notion that our outer being arises from our inner being. Just one of these teachings, but one that I love, is that of the Divine Abidings. Here, we are told that to see things *as they really are* we have to abide well, abiding in loving-kindness, compassion and joy in and for others. These alone will lead to the fourth abiding, equanimity, which will enable us to see clearly. Without them, we cannot truly see.

Over many years, I have wondered about this. And, in other work,[29] I have explored and come to see Love with a capital 'L' as being the shaping energy of all that is. It seems to me that as we begin to understand more and more about the importance of the connection between things, the importance of relationships, we are discovering what might be called 'Love at work'. I don't mean by this Love as sentiment, nor as a virtue, but Love as a mysterious informing *principle of Being* within and beyond us. And even if I cannot define it, I notice it and I experience it. It is there in those things that are closest to me in my everyday life. In close and communal relationships, such as in the café where I have breakfast on Saturday mornings, amongst my friends and family and when I am working with colleagues. When I look for Love, it seems to be there more often than it is not. Indeed, as I look I find a multitude of small acts of kindness and compassion, a care for the other.

Peacefulness begins within you and me, and then extends to those close by. In a world that seems to be ever more divisive, this is a kind of revolution, and one that we are empowered to be part of. For I have discovered that small acts of random kindness can be quite subversive to a culture that denies them.

PEACEFULNESS THROUGH SILENCE AND STILLNESS

In a world of constant chatter, newsfeeds and social media, let alone 'fake news', it might be thought outrageous to suggest that another two components of peacefulness are silence and stillness. The exploration of silence and stillness is part of the work of the Spirit of Humanity Forum,[30] whose press has published this book. The Forum is an organisation based in Iceland, but with a 'community of practitioners' that is spread worldwide. Over recent years, it has deliberately sought to nurture the practise of love, compassion and peacefulness, not only in what is said, but in the manner of its being. For when we have met together to learn from each other, to be inspired and encouraged, we have learnt that certain practices and ways of being give rise to peacefulness. Most importantly, and given the relentless cacophony of the world 'out there', we have learnt the importance of shared stillness and silence.

Again and again, participants in our gatherings have said how this practice has refreshed them; how it has enabled them to see more clearly how they might undertake their work. At first, it seems unlikely that this would happen. We are so used to engaging through words, without any spaces in between, that we think that this anxious and pacey discourse is the only way we will be heard. But it turns out to be otherwise. The gathered silence, the pauses in between, the slowness of discourse, somehow seem to enable people to be listened to. And then the listening seems to become more important than the speaking. We learn to hold the silence so that we can hear, reflect and then, only then, take action. This is the work of peacefulness.

One might suppose that the practise of silence and stillness would be passive, but this is not so. Indeed, the practise holds a deep energy. For some, this is found in meditation, most often some form of sitting or walking meditation, focusing on the in and out rhythm of the breath. For me, the practise is different. Given my Quaker childhood and education, silence and stillness are deeply embedded and are now practised as a continuous background to my being, expressed in a grammar of pauses, commas and full stops, a drawing back into silence wherever and whenever I can. This is similar to the practise of the Brahma Kumaris who, throughout their day, on the hour and sometimes on the half hour, have short periods of stillness and silence. They call it 'traffic control' – pauses of between one and three minutes. Whatever they are doing, they pause for a moment and then continue. This is how they describe it:

> As days become busier in an increasingly busy world, here is a short, practical and empowering exercise which you can integrate into your daily lifestyle. At regular intervals throughout the day, stop whatever you are doing (if practical at that time) and withdraw your attention from everything around you […]
>
> When you stop, bring your attention back to yourself. You will become aware of the heavy traffic of your thoughts passing through your mind. As you start to observe your thoughts they will naturally begin to slow down. Then just remember who you are – a peaceful soul who is master of mind and body. Three minutes spent practising this exercise regularly will enable you to quickly regain concentration, focus and energy which you can then re-direct to whatever you were doing.[31]

To find peacefulness, it seems to be necessary to break the habits of busyness, the having to do and the having to have. In a society such as ours, with its focus on activity and consumption, practising silence and stillness is a subversive action, part of that revolution I was speaking of. It adds nothing to GDP, it requires no kit, nor does it require anyone else to provide it for us. And yet, once it becomes part of our lives, a minute or two at a time, it changes everything. It is the beginning of peacefulness.

PRINCIPLES OF ENLIVENMENT

This brings me to the final part of my proposition. If, as it has been suggested, we are by nature a loving people and if we have in the ancient past lived lives that are rooted in belonging and peacefulness – an alignment with, and an acceptance of, coming to be and ceasing to be, entangled with the rhythms and patterns of Nature and all that is – is it possible that we can in the future become more 'at one' and thereby more peaceful than we are now? Is it even possible that we are witnessing the decline of this long-held culture of fear and division and are moving towards modes of being that are loving and communal? Are we returning to relatedness and wholeness? Is this who we are to become?

Again, I accept that for many this will seem an absurd thing to suggest. After all, there is plenty of evidence that separation and continued violence are prevalent, some of it quite recently so and much of it is still happening as I write. But suppose for a moment that this is no more than the death cries of an old and no longer viable culture and that, at the same time, pushing through the cracks, there are insistent shoots of something else. Something that is changing us. We may not have heard much about it, but that should not be surprising. Amid all the noise and bluster of the dominant ideology, it is unlikely that such a phenomenon would be reported.

Is it possible that a greater and more profound experience of entanglement and wholeness is something not of the past, but of the future, something towards which we may be moving as part of our continuous evolution, our flow of being? If, in the past, there have been but a few sages and mystics who have experienced such oneness, is it possible that this will in time become part of our common being?

One of the reasons we might not be able to envision this is because it requires that we let go of much of our learnt experience, drawn from the philosophical movement called the Enlightenment. This may be difficult to do because the Enlightenment is regarded as an entirely good thing, something that is beyond criticism. The work of the Enlightenment, which began in the latter part of the seventeenth century with what it claimed to be 'rational questioning', was undertaken by breaking things down into their parts so that each part could be better understood. Separation. It was a doctrine that required 'objectivity' – that subject and object should be regarded as separate. Distance. It embraced the notion that everything could be rationally demystified and catalogued. And there can be no doubt that it has provided us with many wonderful things, not least vast improvements in health care and technology.

Nevertheless, more recently, some of the notions of the Enlightenment have been questioned, for example, in Quantum Theory and much of modern physics, where it is not the separation, but the relationship between one thing and another that seems to be important. And one person who has put forward another possibility is the German academic and scholar, Andreas Weber.

In 2013, Weber wrote an essay for the Heinrich Böell Foundation[32] in which he challenged the doctrine of Enlightenment and proposed, instead, the principle of 'Enlivenment':

> A pluralist world of living beings entangled with each other within a biosphere that must be understood as a continuous unfolding of diversity, freedom and experience.[33]

Moving away from a reductionist worldview, Enlivenment envisages a worldview, "that situates human beings deeply in a web of dynamic, living and unfolding creative relationships."[34] It opens the unexplored territory of the nature of life itself, and reveals that subjectivity, sentience, agency, expression, values and autonomy lie at the centre of the biosphere. New sciences are revealing organisms to be sentient, and Enlivenment is, "a way to move beyond our modern metaphysics of 'dead matter' and acknowledge the deeply creative, poetic and expressive processes embodied in all living organisms."[35]

Weber's essay introduces concepts of wholeness, relatedness and community, a form of resilient environment-based systems that he calls 'the commons', even in that presently most holy of holies, 'The Economy', suggesting a new sort of economy that honours people's personal needs and intrinsic interests, "enhancing their sense of aliveness and, in the process, intensifying the aliveness of the underlying ecosystems."[36]

This experience of Enlivenment, with its emphasis upon connectivity and interdependence, is always set within the greater whole of community, the reality of relationships. And yet, as we ponder the meaning of peacefulness, one of Weber's most contentious observations is that the biosphere is not cooperative in a simple, straightforward way, but "paradoxically cooperative":[37]

> Symbiotic relationships emerge out of antagonistic, incompatible processes [...] Incompatibility is needed to achieve life in the first place, and any living existence can only be precarious and preliminary [...] In this sense, living systems are always a self-contradictory 'meshwork of selfless selves'.[38]

The recognition of antagonism and paradox as part of Nature's way may be a useful and helpful insight, preventing us from falling into an unrealistic sentimentality. But, for our present purposes, and in relation to my own claims for a form of wholeness that includes differentiation, it should be noted that Weber goes on to say: "The individual can only exist if the whole exists and the whole can only exist if individuals are allowed to exist."[39]

So, it would seem that the 'antagonistic, incompatible processes' have to be, can only be, resolved within the wellbeing of the whole. Closing the cleft between us and the other, between the part and the whole, is what we too are trying to heal in the quest for peacefulness – the cleft between separation and wholeness, between separation and belonging; being apart from and being together. Here is one scholar who seems to share the possibility that we might be finding our way towards a new awareness of what it means to be whole and diverse, a new and lively entanglement. As I have already said, this is something towards which we may be moving as part of our continuous evolution, our flow of our being.

CONCLUSION

So, where have we come from and where might we be getting to? In claiming the importance of inner being in the quest for peacefulness, I have pointed to realms of wholeness which include differentiation, worlds which we once knew and to which we may, once again, be moving. I have drawn from our most ancient past, Maturana's *Homo sapiens-amans*, traditional teachings of love and peacefulness expressed, not least, in my own Quakerism and then, finally, the proposals now being put forward that seek to 'upgrade' Enlightenment thinking, moving us beyond notions of separation towards notions of inclusion, even entanglement.

Set within such a context, the quest for peacefulness takes a different form than that offered in much of the present peace literature. Instead of being no more than an alternative to war and violence, it becomes a necessary part of what Weber has called 'symbiotic relationships' in which, if living systems are always precarious and self-contradictory, there is a necessary coexistence between individuals and the community and an essential reciprocity between the two.

In this sense, peacefulness is a necessary quality of our manner of being, whether it be in private or public. If it is nurtured from within and then arises in our closest relationships; it is carried 'out there' only if it is supported by appropriate social and economic structures and by what my colleague, Scherto Gill, later in this book refers to as an appropriate communal 'collective intention' or 'communing'. Such a shift in consciousness may be emerging in diverse places, in science, in education, in health care and even in business. The work of the Spirit of Humanity Forum is to provide places in which this shift in consciousness can be felt and expressed, inspired and encouraged.

---

3. Anne Baring and Jules Cashford, 1991, *The Myth of the Goddess: Evolution of an Image*, Viking, 48.

4. Ibid, 79.

5. Ibid.

6. Ibid.

7. Marija Gimbutas, 1982, *The Goddess and Gods of Old Europe, 6500-3500 BC: Myths Cults and Images,* London: Thames and Hudson, Preface.

8. Anne Baring and Jules Cashford, 1991, *The Myth of the Goddess: Evolution of an Image*, Viking, 81-82.

9. Ibid, 82.

10. Ibid, 107.

11. Ibid, 109.

12. Ibid, 132.

13. Ibid, 148.

14. Ibid, 148.

15. Ibid, 132.

16. matriztica.cl.

17. These comments are based upon a sharing of ideas with Simón Ramirez and his colleagues in the Spring of 2017.

18. Humberto Maturana, 1988, 'Reality: The Search for Objectivity or the Quest for a Compelling Argument', *Irish Journal of Psychology* (Issue on Constructivism), 9 (i), 25-82.

19. Humberto Maturana Romesin, Ximena Dávila Yáñez and Simón Ramirez Muñoz, 2015, 'Cultural-Biology, Systemic Consequences of Our Evolutionary Natural Drift as Molecular Autopoetic Systems', *Foundations of Science*, 21 (4), 631-678.

20. Humberto Maturana and Francisco Varela, 1988, *The Tree of Knowledge*, Boston: Shambala New Science Library.

21. Op. cit., Maturana et al., 2015.

22. Discussion with Simón Ramirez and his colleagues in the Spring of 2017.

23. Theodore Zeldin, 1994, *An Intimate History of Humanity*, Sinclair-Stevenson Limited.

24. Discussion with Simón Ramirez and his colleagues in the Spring of 2017.

25. Humberto Maturana, Edited by J C Saez, 2008, *Habitar Humano en seis ensayos de Biología-Cultural (Human Living: Six Essays on Cultural Biology), Castellano.*

26. Matthew 5:44.

27. *Quaker Faith & Practice*, Fourth Edition, Yearly meeting of the Religious Society of Friends (Quakers) in Britain, 2009, 24.03.

28. Ibid, 1.02.

29. See, for example, David Cadman, 2014, *Love Matters*, Zig Publishing, and Scherto Gill and David Cadman, 2016, *Why Love Matters*, Peter Lang.

30. sohforum.org.

31. These words are taken from the old website of the Brahma Kumaris. The new website: brahmakaris.org/meditation/time-for-meditation refers to the practice of traffic control.

32. Andreas Weber, 2013, *Enlivenment: Towards a Fundamental Shift in the Concepts of Nature, Culture and Politics*, Heinrich Böell Foundation, www.boell.de.

33. Dr Heike Löschmann in the Foreword to the essay, ibid, 7.

34. Ibid.

35. Ibid.

36. Ibid, 8.

37. Ibid, 32.

38. Ibid.

39. Ibid.

CHAPTER **TWO**

TOWARDS INNER-OUTER PEACE: CULTIVATING SPIRITUALITY AND RELATIONSHIP

MAUREEN GOODMAN

ASKED TO CONSIDER THE CONNECTION between inner and outer peacefulness, I have reflected on that which I know best – my own work within the Brahma Kumaris and the work of my sisters and brothers. What I wish to show, by reflection and reference to practical work, is that outer peacefulness arises from peace within. They are intertwined. This relationship is based on the spiritual principle that whatever is within is reflected without – the inner state of human beings creates the outer state of the world.

During my most recent visit to India, I witnessed a project showing spirituality in action. I visited the site of India One,[40] a thermal solar power plant that had just become operational. It had been completed, against all odds, by people who learned their expertise as they went along. They had purpose, vision, will and, above all else, they had community. They gained the support of the Indian and German governments and are now supplying electricity to thousands of people. The site has also been designated a Training Centre on Concentrating Solar Thermal Technologies under the United Nations Development Programme. I had made several visits over the six years that it took to build, and I reflected on how I saw a community of people coming together both for an immediate task, and also to do something for the world. Now that the plant is operational, I cannot describe the light in their faces. Their 'power of community' made what could have been an arduous task into a joy.

There is a principle at work here – the sense of purpose among the initiators of this project brought them an inner tranquillity and certainty that created an atmosphere which engendered cooperation. Inner peace is felt as a vibration that gently overpowers the resistance of negativity. Inner peace is not just related to having peaceful thoughts and feelings, but also to an inner knowing that I am fulfilling my purpose and allowing the inner voice of my conscience to guide me.

In the quest for peacefulness, we are looking here at a paradigm for transformation that is rooted in a spiritual awareness and works from the inside out. It has several aspects: an awareness of the original state of peace of our being; an awareness of a greater source than ourselves upon which we can draw; an awareness of being part of the greater whole, and a vision of a future without suffering. These aspects are completely interconnected and necessary for us to move forward. They are based on what my colleague, Sister Jayanti, has called, "The spiritual truth which is a basic principle, that whatever is within is reflected without. The inner state of human beings creates the outer state of the world."[41]

When we consider the problems our planet is facing right now, it is clear that the power of the human spirit must lead in healing and transformation. The Earth Charter, recognises that, "peace is the wholeness created by right relationships with oneself, other persons, other cultures, other life, Earth, and the larger whole of which all are a part."[42] These 'right relationships' are, in turn, a reflection of our connection with the Source, the Divine.

RELATIONSHIPS WITH ONESELF AND OTHERS

So often in our teachings we are told if someone is angry with you, stay quiet, not just externally, but also internally. We do not have to battle with negativity, but we need to continue to create positivity within as that will generate an atmosphere of peace around us. If we continue to have thoughts of anger or even irritation, resistance is still created. I have experienced the power of peace working on many occasions. Dadi Janki, the head of the Brahma Kumaris, has an incredible presence of peace after 80 years or more of practising meditation (as I write this she is 101 years of age). Once she was sharing, with her usual enthusiasm, and one woman in the crowded room was getting increasingly upset. Eventually, she burst out, "What right have you to be happy when I am so miserable!" Dadi paused and, with a deep sense of peace and love said to her, "If I also become unhappy and peaceless, who would there be to bring you peace and happiness?" That sentence changed that woman's life.

We often find ourselves in situations where we begin to judge, criticise or blame. Even if we do not speak of it, we think it, sometimes to the extent of it becoming an obsession. The moment we return to a state of inner peace that is independent of the influence of others, we have also achieved real inner power. A peaceful mind is no longer reactive, but rather proactive: we choose peace, choose goodness. This completely changes the dynamic of a relationship.

Returning to this state of inner peace again and again has a profound effect upon behaviour. A practising meditator, who was working as a psychiatrist in a busy hospital in London, described her experience to me. She was called out to deal with a patient who refused to take his medicine. She calmly handed him his medicine and the patient became agitated and being much taller than her, tipped it over her head. She then went in to a deep state of inner peace. The patient visibly calmed down and, within a few minutes, accepted his medicine. That psychiatrist is now working on developing a phone app which contains tools for health care practitioners in times of high stress.

How we relate to each other is perhaps the greatest litmus test of what we are really feeling inside. If you say that you 'love the world', but you fight with your sister or brother or cannot get on with your neighbour, then that statement becomes meaningless. At that moment, it is important to ask, how much do I love my own self? To love myself is to understand and believe in my inherent value as a human being. Every thought we have and every breath we take is valuable. Dadi Janki speaks of the deep inter-connection between our thoughts, our breath and our energy. We breathe according to the quality of our thoughts. Our breath provides the energy for our interaction in the world. So, our actions are an expression of our innermost thoughts or the subtle intention in our being.

So, for me, the challenge is to keep the awareness of my own original state of peace and to also recognise and relate to that in the other. I have to see through the personality in front of me to a new possibility for that person. Thomas Hübl, a contemporary spiritual teacher, said, "If you say that you know someone, then that is laziness." In other words, we slip into an old habit of relating to that person as they have been previously, even just yesterday. It is necessary to make the extra effort of putting aside old impressions and being present to make the relationship anew.

RELATIONSHIP WITH SOCIETY

In terms of the wider society, inner peace is like a seed that bears a variety of fruits as outer expressions in the world. The seed, although no longer visible, is still a part of the fruit. We have several 'seeds' within us. Peace brings contentment, patience, clarity and stability. Love brings care, compassion, nurture and healing. Wisdom brings understanding, justice, equality and fearlessness. Joy brings courage, enthusiasm, kindness and hope. There are many more examples that could be given, but nurturing the seed is important for the fruit to flourish. Very often, *how* we do is as important as *what* we do.

In 2001, there was a devastating earthquake in Bhuj, India. One of our sisters told me a story of her time doing relief work. As she was distributing raw food and cooking apparatus to those who just a day before had everything and now had nothing, she was told, "When you give to us, we do not feel that we lose our dignity." I reflected on this. When one gives to a family member, it is a natural give and take, not a handout given out of pity. She had the natural awareness that we are all part of one human family. So, in relating to others, our feelings and intentions have a big impact. We are serving others to take away their fear and give them hope.

It was his deep inner search and sense of purpose that led Brahma Baba, the founder of the Brahma Kumaris, to challenge the status quo in 1930s India by putting women at the forefront as spiritual leaders and teachers. As with all great spiritual people, he knew that the more powerful the transformation is within, the greater will be the impact without. To this day, the leadership of the Brahma Kumaris is in the hands of women, working in partnership with men. This role reversal was not superficial. Brahma Baba enabled the women, most of whom had very little education, to empower themselves spiritually so that the power was in their hands – they were not followers of another. They have been able to maximise their potential as human beings on this Earth. He gave them true independence. Under their leadership over the past 40 years, the organisation has spread into over 100 countries. If you were to ask any of those women, who are now in their eighties and nineties and more about this, they would always say that we create leaders, never followers. From the very early days, the foundation of their practise has been returning to and nurturing their original state of peace.

RELATIONSHIP WITH THE WORLD

Peace is deeply connected with development. In peace time, societies can flourish; in war, resources are redirected to armaments at the cost of education, health care and many other basic rights. If we look at the root causes of violence, it is because fear has replaced inner peace. Those who are fearful can easily become defensive or even aggressive – their world shrinks. The build-up of fear and insecurity around issues of identity, scarce resources, or land creates the conditions for war.

At present, we see a polarity developing; it is as if the old paradigm is breaking up and a new one is emerging. There is a lot of violence in the world. However, it is a spiritual principle that if you respond to violence with more violence, then a cycle of violence results and the atmosphere of violence becomes more prevalent in society.

There are several leaders who have had the courage to address this principle. Less than two weeks after an attack at a Christmas market in Berlin, German Chancellor, Angela Merkel, spoke of responding to terrorism with compassion:

> I think we could feel it [confidence] here in Berlin and in many other German cities, even in these difficult days – in the comfort that we were able to give or to receive. And in our firm determination to counter the terrorists' hate with our compassion and our solidarity.

Such a statement takes immense courage in a world where many are cowed by fear. Decisions made out of fear only perpetuate negative situations; decisions made out of love and compassion provide hope.

Sister Jayanti expressed similar sentiments after a recent terrorist attack in London:

> Everyone needs peace, and the country needs to be able to trust again. Trust that staying true to our highest values is the best means of safety. When values such as nonviolence, selflessness and generosity of spirit are visible in our

decision-making and in our way of living, it brings a reciprocal response. What we can do is to serve others with love, purity of spirit and peace, rather than to blame. Everyone needs peace.

Such perspectives are not always popular, but as Dadi Janki says in her book, *Wings of Soul*:

> To truly contribute to the process of setting the world right you need to develop a lot of inner, personal power. This is because the path of someone who is trying to do something for the world will always be strewn with obstacles. [...] Often it will only be your faith, courage and honesty that will enable you to carry on.[43]

In returning to the paradigm that will bring about a peaceful world, I would like to explore several key aspects in more depth.

AWARENESS OF OUR ORIGINAL STATE OF PEACE

There is a profound relationship between inner peace, inner power and identity. First of all, it is important to realise that peace is the original state of our being. It is the very nature of the being within, the soul. However, most people identify with their physical, outer aspects; how they look, what they do, what they have, how others see them. As physical reality changes – as it inevitably does – so our inner feelings fluctuate and it is difficult to experience inner peace. As a result, we can only be content to the extent that others are content with us. We will not have a constant or stable self-awareness and will not feel 'in charge' of our thoughts or feelings. This then weakens our resolve and makes discernment and decision-making difficult.

With a truer self-awareness, we can acknowledge the constant being within, a self that is non-physical, a form of consciousness or soul. This alters our perception of ourselves and the world. We are no longer simply reflecting what the world projects on to us – living from the outside in; instead we are now being present in the world as we are – living from the inside out.

The moment we begin to free ourselves from the influence of the personality, opinions, needs of others and of our own ego, it clears the space for an awareness of who we really are. As we reflect on this, we begin to experience our own inner state of peace that was previously masked by our fears. We begin to understand the true nature of our being, that of peace, love, wisdom and joy. This is no longer just a theory – it becomes our experience. These qualities give us immense inner power. The power to grow these qualities within and to regain our dignity and self-sovereignty. We begin to flourish as human beings. Real power is, therefore, not power over someone else, but power over oneself; mastery over our own thoughts and feelings based on experiencing our true identity.

So, how does this manifest in the world and in my life? My conscience awakens; I begin to live from truth rather than from ego; I am more able to love unconditionally; I begin to see others with an equal vision; my relationships deepen and there is a meeting of hearts; I have greater clarity as to what I have to do in any situation; and my life's purpose becomes increasingly clear to me.

To develop this, I need one thing – time for inner silence. Inner silence means that my thoughts are no longer connected with the outer world – people, places, possessions, whether of the past or present. My thoughts are connected with my innate qualities. I experience the foundation for transformation, a deep inner peace that is stable and strong. Just one thought, 'I am a being of peace', has a profound effect on me – I become that truth. This is a silent contemplation that I can do anywhere at any time. But it is also important to make time, preferably at the beginning and end of the day, to practise this awareness. Eventually, it becomes more and more my natural state of being. I am returning to my original state of wholeness; my original state of peace.

Taking time for the self in this way is not selfish for it requires us to move beyond our own needs to think of the greater good of all. It lifts us up from the influence of the expectations of others to a greater awareness of true human dignity. It switches our *modus operandi* from one of taking from life to the generosity of giving. Peace does not have any boundaries; peace is for everyone.

AWARENESS OF A GREATER SOURCE THAN OURSELVES UPON WHICH WE CAN DRAW

> God acts through others to accomplish things in the world. And those who carry out the actions are called instruments. [...] With the feeling of being an instrument, you automatically have the stage of humility. Why? Because your experience is that the act is being accomplished by something bigger than yourself.[44]

This awareness of 'being an instrument' is behind many great accomplishments in the world. People often feel they are compelled to do something, to extend themselves beyond what appears to be their capacity. This is only possible with God's help.

Sometimes, people are hesitant to speak about their relationship with God. However, because it is a meaningful relationship for so many, I feel we need to acknowledge it in society. I began relying on the Divine to guide me right from my student days, and my relationship with it has continued to grow ever stronger and more fulfilling. And this is what I have found: God is a source of peace, love, strength, joy and truth. The Divine is a constant, eternal source that brings much-needed healing and transformational energy to our world. My connection to the Divine is a connection of the spirit, or consciousness.

As mentioned earlier, a truer self-awareness is of the constant being within, the soul within. Although our relationship with the physical world gives the soul expression, at our essence, we are not physical. In this non-physical awareness, it becomes possible to connect with the Being that is greater than ourselves. In the realm of consciousness, I am not bound by space and time. This is a deeper contemplation that takes me right away from everyday awareness into a deep state of silence where I can fill up my consciousness with Divine energy. It is a gentle and loving experience that I grow to trust more and more. This is a natural connection that we have forgotten. It is not new; it is our original relationship that is comforting, protective and secure. As Neville Hodgkinson has said, "The challenge we have is to allow ourselves to open up to this divine love and wisdom, in order to restore our own loving nature to its full expression."[45]

This is the relationship that Dadi Janki describes in terms of being an instrument. We have spent too long trying to do everything ourselves. We trust our own rational minds more than the love of God and this has not been helpful to our world. She also describes the way instruments work:

> It is as if they have quietly surrendered inside to this higher force that is touching them and have allowed their every step to be guided by this touching. This is why we must continuously live with an openness to these touchings and signals from a higher source.[46]

With the awareness of being an instrument, we can be of service to the world in even the smallest task. This is because we all, wherever we are, continually live off each other's vibrations. Just as the well-known 'Butterfly Effect' of Chaos Theory suggests a butterfly flapping its wings in Brazil has the power to cause a tornado in Texas, our thoughts and feelings produce vibrations that create the atmosphere of the world. The quality of our thoughts and feelings depends very much on our awareness. The more we live in the awareness of our original state of peace, the more healing and powerful our vibrations become. We need to build up the power of good, healing, vibrations in our world. Our inner peace ensures that there is no interference in the work of those vibrations.

The more we connect with the Divine as instruments and are guided by the highest truth, the more powerful those vibrations will be. It is as if we fill each thought with a greater capacity to be effective. Most of us cannot go away to a forest or a cave to develop this capacity and so need to find a way of doing it, even as we continue with our everyday tasks. In fact, to do this in the midst of our full lives is a greater challenge and actually a more powerful achievement.

An instrument for God will not stray from the path of truth. He or she will endeavour to live in each moment with honesty, with themselves, the Divine and those around them. Truth is connected to the state of purity of being, which brings the most profound state of inner peace. In this original state, anything that is false no longer has any influence. Dadi Janki talks about this in her book, *Inside Out*:

Purity and truth are different states. Purity means free from impurities. Truth means whole, without deception or falsehood. When thought is pure, it enables my life to be truthful and valuable and my potential as a human being to be fulfilled. Purity clears a path for truth. It makes space inside my mind in which truth can be experienced. Purity within the soul is essential for peace.[47]

What is described above *is* the paradigm for transformation that is rooted in our being. This state of being has a profound effect on our relationships with each other and with the natural world around us. The way of purity is the way of peace.

AWARENESS OF BEING PART OF THE GREATER WHOLE

Often, we are faced with those whose intentions towards us or others are not good. At that moment, we need to ask ourselves, "What is the most productive thing to do?" If we speak or act with any kind of hatred, fear or anger, then our vibrations are fuelling their negativity. It takes a lot of inner strength to *not* succumb to righteous anger, but rather to offer the hand of forgiveness and love. The Forgiveness Project in the UK uses real stories of victims and perpetrators to explore the concept of forgiveness, and to encourage people to seek alternatives to resentment, retaliation and revenge. As one woman whose husband was killed in 9/11 says, "Choosing the path to stop the cycle of violence is just as difficult as choosing the other path of anger and hatred."[48]

We are part of one family of humanity and, in smaller ways, part of our own family or community. Families are also communities. Communities of all kinds are now at the vanguard of change. To sustain the momentum for change, peace is required, which allows tolerance, patience and coop-eration. This involves a letting go and forgiveness, so that we can embrace the future together. This willingness to let go of the past harnesses a huge amount of energy and human potential. If we trust in the Divine, we no longer need to carry the burden of a task and we will be open to a new way of being.

This is my own current practice: to be with someone and to listen and, only then, respond. Otherwise, I immediately start a commentary in my head that interprets or judges what the other person is saying, or I am already deciding my answer or point of view. To be open is to bring honesty into my relationships. It also prevents me from becoming obsessed with another person's weaknesses. It helps me to understand. This is the transformative power of love in its simplest and most profound sense. It is something we can do every day and, like the butterfly, it will have a far-reaching effect. We have to recognise that love is the greatest transformative power in the world.

As we transform our consciousness in this practical way, we also transform our relationship with nature. There is a flow of energy from the Divine to the inner being of the self, to those around me and to the physical world. Our closest relationship is with the physical matter of our own body, and this responds immediately to our state of awareness. We have long been aware of the connection between the mind and health. Science now shows us in even greater detail how the very cells of our bodies respond to different states of mind.

In the Brahma Kumaris contribution to the UN Climate Change Conference in Copenhagen in 2009, our relationship with the wider environment is described as the confluence of two living systems – the living system of Nature and the living system of thought. Our paper quoted the late David Bohm, a distinguished theoretician and physicist, who explained that at the root of change is the living system of thought, and that this is participatory – it affects the world, all the while claiming that it is only commenting on the world.

> Thought is always doing a great deal, but it tends to say that it hasn't done anything, that it is just telling you the way things are. But thought affects everything. Even the South Pole has been affected because of the destruction of the ozone layer, which is basically due to thought. People thought that they wanted to have refrigerant – a nice safe refrigerant – and they built that all up by thinking more and more about it. And now we have the ozone layer being destroyed.[49]

Identifying the cause of the damage led to the Montreal Protocol (an international treaty that phased out the production of CFCs globally) and the gradual reversal of ozone layer depletion – again, a result of thought.

We have a responsibility to the greater whole. Ultimately, peace in our being manifests as thoughts that bring harmony and alignment. Thoughts are the seeds of change. The natural world needs the power of peace. This is a great gift to the world.

A VISION OF A FUTURE WITHOUT SUFFERING

Our inner state of peace lays the foundation for a better world. By transforming our thinking and infusing each thought with peace, we will achieve wisdom in our decision-making. Wisdom is inclusive – it does not discriminate, it does not undermine and it creates a beneficial outcome for all. It does not work from the false ego, but, rather, brings forth the expression of the true inner being. As we develop our organisational structures, governance systems and ways of working from this deeper awareness, a new paradigm that is compassionate and caring begins to show itself. Many are working towards this in our world today.

Earlier, I referred to the elder sisters of the Brahma Kumaris, the 'Dadis'. I have learned a lot from witnessing their wise leadership. They would begin and close each meeting with a few minutes of silence and also stop for a few minutes of silence in between. This enables everyone present to think and speak from their original state of being, avoiding any selfish motives, connecting with the Divine and maintaining an atmosphere of respect. At our centres, we also have the practice of stopping whatever we are doing for a minute every hour to reconnect, harmonise our vibrations and make use of our time most effectively. Over many years now, I have watched how the Dadis would repeatedly put the welfare of individuals first, knowing that in this is the welfare of all. At the same time, they would encourage us to think of the good of everyone in our decision-making. They are very inclusive. They make decisions by consensus – I have hardly ever had to vote in a meeting! They give respect to the ideas and opinions of all, be they young, old, rich or poor, always encouraging young people to come forward to shoulder responsibility. They keep the awareness of being an instrument, they maintain humility and are fearless in following the path of truth.

Courage and fearlessness are necessary for holding a vision for the future and providing hope for humanity. In his book, *Point of Departure*, Four Arrows describes courage:

> The highest expression of courage in indigenous worldviews is generosity. Generosity is the manifestation of love. […] courage means the strength of spirit that enables people to accept the unavoidable tragedies of life without being disintegrated. It implies the readiness and willingness to take reasonable risks for the good of family and community.[50]

It is very important to understand courage in this way; not the courage to fight or to oppose, but the courage to use virtue, to use our inner state of peace.

Through our awareness, thoughts, vibrations and consequent actions, we are literally writing a new story for humanity. We are the story. And, as instruments, we have unlimited help from the Divine. As we transition to a better world, we will need great inner strength to trust and hold that vision.

In the 1980s, the Brahma Kumaris began organising international projects, working as an NGO affiliated with the United Nations. The second of these, Global Cooperation for a Better World, asked people of all walks of life for their vision of a better world, which was to be expressed in a positive way. The idea was to harness the power of positivity for change:

> To think, to hope and to dream are abilities enjoyed by people throughout the world, regardless of culture, gender, race or social status. In improving ourselves – and thus the world – the first step is to recognise the unbreakable links between our inner world of ideas, thoughts, and concepts, and the external world of events and circumstance. Just because our world is so volatile and changeable is no need for

despair. Quite the contrary, for the reason why we now live in a world that is changing more rapidly than at any other time in human history, is precisely because individuals have unprecedented power.[51]

There is an increasing awareness of the power available to us and the task ahead is to make sure that we harness spiritual power, rather than the power of ego and position, and that power is used only for the common good of the world. The late Leticia Ramos Shahani, a former senator in the Philippines, understood the need to connect the personal and public spheres:

> Whatever the level of economic growth, countries must maintain in their very societies, values such as respect for individual dignity, accountability in public office, and discipline in community life. The values required [...] are essentially the same for the public and private spheres: truthfulness, honesty and the transcendence of the spiritual side of life.[52]

Senator Shahani is telling us that values are the interface between the state of our being and our decisions and actions. The blueprint of change then becomes clearer. In our original state of peace, we open our hearts and minds to listen to our deepest selves and to the Divine, and become instruments for God's healing and transformative energy to come to the Earth. We need to translate that energy into the wisdom of spirituality, making the highest values the foundation of our decision-making. We need the courage to put ourselves at the heart of society as instruments for change, and believe in our vision for a world of happiness for all.

Without the power of silence, this would seem impossible. As we spend time in silence, our inner power builds, we begin to see a true spiritual reality, we value our thoughts, words, actions and time, and we use them effectively and with happiness. We are in touch with our conscience, we return to our original state of peace. As instruments of the Divine, in silence, we create a world without suffering.

CONCLUSION

In this chapter, I have described the deep connection of inner and outer peace. We have seen the effect that the power of our original state of peace has on our thoughts, awareness, values, decisions and actions; how our being in a state of inner peace is the foundation of the transformational paradigm that can bring about a peaceful world. And, above all, we have emphasised the daily practice of inner silence as the way to make such change possible.

I leave you with a story of hope:

> A gigantic fire broke out in the jungle. The animals flocked together on the other side of the lake and they gazed at the flames. A small bird, seeing what was going on, took a drop of water in its little beak and let it drop on the flames. It returned, took another little drop in its beak and let it fall. And like this it flew back and forth diligently. The rest of the animals just watched him and said to each other, "And what does this one think he can actually do with his little drop of water?" At one stage they asked him, "Tell us, little bird, do you honestly believe you can put out the fire with your little drop of water?" The little bird answered, "I do what I must." Just then an angel went by, saw the little bird and produced a great rainfall. The fire went out.[53]

40.   http://www.india-one.net/

41.   Sister Jayanti, Keynote Address, May, 2001, Conference on Promoting Prevention of Violent Conflict and Building Peace by Interaction between State Actors and Voluntary Organisations, Sweden.

42.   http://earthcharter.org/discover/the-earth-charter/

43.   Dadi Janki, *Wings of Soul*, 1999, Health Communications Inc.

44.   J Rogers and G Naraine, 2009, *Something Beyond Greatness*, Health Communications Inc.

45.   Neville Hodgkinson, 2015, *I Know How To Live, I Know How to Die*, Mantra Books.

46.   J Rogers and G Naraine, 2009, *Something Beyond Greatness*, Health Communications Inc.

47. Dadi Janki, 2013, *Inside Out: A Better Way of Living, Learning and Loving,* BKIS.

48. http://theforgivenessproject.com/

49. David Bohm, 1994, *Thought as a System*, London: Routledge.

50. Four Arrows, 2016, *Point of Departure*, USA: IAP.

51. *Visions of a Better World*, 1993, A UN Peace Messenger Publication, Brahma Kumaris.

52. Ibid.

53. *Visions of a Better World*, 1993, A UN Peace Messenger Publication, Brahma Kumaris.

CHAPTER **THREE**

PEACE WITHIN ONESELF AND ALL OF CREATION – AN INDIGENOUS PERSPECTIVE

FOUR ARROWS (A.K.A. DON TRENT JACOBS)

ALTHOUGH THIS LAKOTA WORD, *WOLOKOLKICIAPI,* might be defined by the title of this chapter, the translation is insufficient to capture what it truly means to the people whose language stems from the landscape of their ancestors. Nonetheless, it serves here as a guide for understanding the idea of inner peacefulness. It helps teach us about what conditions can bring us to it and then how to breathe it into all our relations. It offers a teaching for realising a way of being in the world that guided human beings for most of our history on this planet, in spite of what history books have taught us. The energy in the vibrations of this term might lead us into our own versions of the lifeways of our Indigenous ancestors and of those who have, against all odds, managed to hold on to them.

AN INDIGENOUS UNDERSTANDING OF PEACE

Various Indigenous cosmologies express what it means to be human. They vary from culture to culture, but they are generally based on the belief that there is a spiritual force in the universe that permeates all that exists. Each person's mission, then, is to live in harmony with how this force expresses itself in the visible and invisible energies that dwell in a particular place. The ability to focus on and learn from the relationships in one's own environment in order to live in balance is what being Indigenous is all about. This ability then can be expanded throughout the universe as *wolocolkiciapi.*

Building on the wisdom of people who lived in an area prior to colonisation, Indigenous people today – that is, those with authentic ties or identifications with this 'original' understanding – struggle to hold on to this wisdom. Although colonisation and the dominant worldview that separates humans from the natural world have undermined this understanding for thousands of years, more and more people are now starting to recognise it, and want to learn about it and protect it.

However, walking a path of harmony is not an easy a task. It is especially difficult for humans compared to other life forms. I am not sure why this is, but I think it has to do with how easily we can use our most powerful abilities for surviving and thriving to destroy ourselves. For example, our unique talent for imagining can too easily be used to deceive ourselves.

From this, we have lost our sense of interconnectedness with all and have created a hierarchy over Nature that is unnatural in many ways. In 2010, in a peer-reviewed article co-authored by my daughter and grandson, I described how we can rediscover how plants and animals can help us prevent such misguided behaviours.[54]

This is why, for Indigenous peoples, non-human lifeforms are considered to be our teachers. Walking a path to learn this way requires a courage (*wohetike*) and respectfulness that gives significance to the self and to all that is other than oneself (*wowayuonihan*). Nonetheless, living in harmony with all our relations, both human and non-human, has been a powerful goal of all primal cultures. It is sustained by observations of the complementarity, symbiosis and interconnectivity present in natural systems. The Lakota refer to this journey towards harmony as walking along 'the red road' or *chanku luta*. The way of being in the world that results from *chanku luta* is *wolokolkiciapi* – peace within oneself and with all of creation.

Such an effort to live life this way was practised under the worldview that guided humanity for 99% of our time on this planet. In spite of schooling, academic books, media and folklore's attempts to suggest otherwise, this worldview and its diverse cosmological representations did lead to peaceful relationships.[55] As this book sets out to question such hegemony and to show that a negative conception of ourselves is itself a barrier to peace, it is thus important to counter the messages that teach us that humans are intrinsically warlike, and, indeed, there are significant studies that prove otherwise. Unfortunately, such scholarship rarely makes it into mainstream publications because of the established hegemony.[56] Indeed, Dennen writes in *Origins of War*:

> I shall argue that the claim of universal human belligerence is grossly exaggerated; and that those students who have been developing theories of war, proceeding from the premise that peace is the 'normal' situation, have not been erring nincompoops or starry-eyed utopians; and that peace – the continuation of potentially conflictious interactions between discernible groups of human beings with other means – in primitive peoples is just as much a deliberate and

conscious and rational political strategy, based on cost/
benefit considerations and ethical judgments, as is war.[57]

This normalcy of peacefulness in human groups and communities is likewise recognised by other scholars. For instance, Leavitt's classic study[58] is
one of many that show war was absent or rare in 73% of hunter-gatherer
societies. Equally, in 1915, Hobhouse, Wheeler, and Ginsberg concluded
their extensive study of 650 'primitive' peoples, saying:

> The question has been raised whether the traditional view of
> early society as one of constant warfare is really justified by
> the facts. There is, in fact, no doubt that to speak of a state
> of war as normal is in general a gross exaggeration.[59]

Then, in 1956, Hobhouse supported this finding in the *British Journal of
Sociology*.[60] On the University of Alabama's prestigious Department of
Anthropology website is a list of the 25 most peaceful societies today for
whom scholarly studies show the consistent ability to effectively foster
interpersonal harmony and which rarely permit violence or warfare in their
lives. All but one, the Amish, are surviving Indigenous cultures. Most
have a significantly deep relationship with their natural environment. It
is not a coincidence that 80% of the biodiversity on Earth is on the 20%
of landmass still occupied by Indigenous peoples.

When people say that such societies are peaceful because they are primitive,
I reply that it is to the contrary. I say it is more likely that they are primitive
because they are peaceful. War is adaptive to an anthropocentric, material-
istic worldview, one focused on hierarchy and profit that began when we
started waging war against Nature. The impact of war is not only tragic as
it relates to the loss of human life, but also because of destruction to the
environment. When Nature, and harmony with it, are appreciated and
prioritised, people tend to make lifestyle choices that are less negatively
impactful to their environments.[61] To make peace with ourselves then is to
make peace with all of Nature, recognising that we are part of it. From the
Indigenous perspective, this begins with establishing a relationship with the
energies surrounding the particular environment one finds oneself occupying.
It works because such a relationship reveals that Nature is a representation

of harmony. We can do this today, even without the benefit of the wisdom of the ages in places where Indigenous peoples no longer dwell.

Of course, many people do not see Nature in the way I am describing. Many see it as a representation of violence, an idea often considered to be the opposite of peace. However, from the Indigenous perspective, peacefulness is not mere tranquillity, or an absence of forceful action. 'Violence', depending how one defines it, can be complementary to peace. For example, consider the violence of a storm. It works in harmony with the quiet before it and the refreshing calm after it. Its intentions are ultimately about flowing balance and healthfulness. If we use the more common definition where violence is intentional hurtfulness (as in war or domestic violence), anger, or a villainous motivation comes before and suffering follows. The idea of *wolokolkiciapi* allows for Nature's violence or fierceness, which is never malicious, jealous, angry or fearful. It is accepting of the intense forces of Nature and understands its part in purifying, healing and offering mutual aid in the long run. It is about a continual giving of significance and relatedness to all. It sees humour, love, and beauty in the natural struggle for survival.

Thus, peace is not perfection. Nor is it individualistic. It is ultimately about the whole. It sees the Earth as a microcosm of the universe. It sees the human body as a microcosm of the Earth. Perhaps contemplative practices and spiritual traditions like yoga or tai chi may have emerged when Indigenous worldviews became overshadowed and God seemed to move indoors. Wise elders might have realised it was more difficult to achieve peacefulness (*wolokolkiciapi*) in the cities that had replaced more natural environments, but they knew that a focus on harmonising the body/mind/spirit might lead to the more holistic orientation of a life in balance.

Seeing the human body as a metaphor for place is still a powerful way to rekindle the gentle flames and cool water that are the strength of *wolokolkiciapi*. Of course, seeing the human body as a metaphor for place has long been a part of Indigenous spiritual understandings, even when immersed in the natural world. Greg Cajete, a noted Tewa author and director of Native Studies at the University of New Mexico, writes in his classic text, the *Natural Laws of Independence* that, "Native cultures talk, pray and chant the landscape into their being" when living in "the place Indian people talk about."[62] He explains that the psychology and spirituality that inspired the ability to harmonise with all relationships was:

> Thoroughly 'in-formed' by the depth and power of their participation mystique with the Earth as a living soul. It was from this orientation that Indian people developed 'responsibilities' to the land and all living things [...] Spirit and matter were not separate; they were one and the same.[63]

This may be why, in spite of what revisionist history tells us, pre-contact Indigenous peoples treated their own bodies with such reverence and were noted for their fitness, hygiene and holistic wellness.

Practices such as those in various yogic traditions allow one to work towards a mystical participation with the Earth by working on one's body/mind/ spirit, which is a mirror of it, even within doors and apart from the outside world. Cajete writes that:

> Since yoga is a form of energetic and spiritual exercise like tai chi [...] I would say yes, it develops empathy with your body and the world at the same time [...] this would be especially true if it is done in the natural world and on the ground [...]. This is why native ceremonies are done outside or in a structure like a *hogan* or *kiva* connected to the earth and made of the earth.[64]

Thus, with the intentionality that connects personal body/mind/spirit work with the 'Oneness of All' and the deep respect for the gift of life on Earth, we can re-envision our appropriate responsibilities to the land, even when we are not necessarily where we can interrelate with the living soul in Nature, such as near trees or rivers – although, even in big cities, one can usually find other-than or more-than human entities with which to interact. Imagine that each of us starts with our own commitment to the harmony of our body/mind/spirit, and then we connect this to our local place and the community that occupies it, and realise the interconnectedness with all! This may well be a stimulus for transformation.

However, this has not proven to be enough if the state of our world today is taken as evidence. I wish, therefore, to offer two specific ways the Indigenous perspective might help with this process, beyond the vital need to start with one's own body/mind/spirit self. These are: (1) Seeking complementarity, and (2) Trance-based learning with self-hypnotic techniques.

SEEKING COMPLEMENTARITY

Complementary relationships are an essential reality in Nature and thus a major assumption of the Indigenous worldview. Rather than distinguishing between opposites, such as the sacred and the profane, the religious and the secular, mind and body, human beings and Nature, the Indigenous regards these paired opposites as complimentary dualities. Although such thinking in terms of opposites seems to be a worldwide practice in all cultures, problems arise when the tension between the opposite remains rigidly polarised. Jung writes that Western cultures tend to ignore, repress or keep separate psychological or relational opposites, and he thought this practice was dysfunctional for both individuals and societies:

> Unfortunately, our Western mind, lacking all culture in this respect, has never yet devised a concept, nor even name, for the union of opposites through the middle path, that most fundamental item of inward experience […].[65]

Instead, the tension of opposites is avoided or even destroyed, which is not a healthy way to live in a world full of natural dualities that ultimately work together for the greater good.

How to see mutual aid in binaries has long been a theme in the twin hero myths that abound throughout the world. They are usually about the contrasting, yet complementary energies of the sun and the moon. One twin is powerful, physically strong and direct like the sun's rays. The other is passive, mentally strong and reflective or indirect like the dynamics of the moon. In Indigenous stories, twin heroes like the Navajo's 'Child Born of the Water' and 'Monster Slayer', work together in harmony on the journey to rid the world of its demons.

However, the emergence of monotheism and patriarchy in Middle Eastern religions tended to mute this type of duality, obscuring the more 'feminine' principle. In fact, this is essentially the position of Shepard, who writes about the great departure from the Nature-based Indigenous worldview:

> Its true genesis lies in the work of Hebrew and Greek demythologizers. They created a reality focused outside the self, one that could be manipulated the way god-the-potter fingered the world.[66]

This happened, for example, when the solar twin, Romulus, actually murders his lunar brother, Remus. Hercules, the quintessential patriarchal solar hero, was born with a lunar twin named Iphicles that few of us remember. And in the biblical story of Jacob and Esau, Jacob steals Esau's birthright and tries to enslave him. Esau, the trickster brother who is close to all animals, especially the water animals, is obviously the lunar twin.

Such mythological change from the Indigenous to the Greek and Roman ways of telling the twin hero stories may show how deeply ingrained our separation from Nature really is. More importantly, it shows we have a choice. We can live according to the belief that we are part of Nature intrinsically, physically and spiritually. We can acknowledge the proven assumptions gleaned after over a million years of surviving and thriving on Earth. Or, we can live according to a belief that we are somehow separate from the Earth and its life systems, while continuing to ignore, dismiss or ridicule our Indigenous wisdom. The evidence is clear for choosing which of these foundational beliefs will best serve future generations.

TRANCE-BASED LEARNING

For most of us, making the choice to seek complementarity between apparent opposites cannot just be something that happens as a result of wilful determination. The dominant worldview is too embedded in our psyche. I contend that it is only by understanding the phenomenon of trance-based learning that we can explain what we, as intelligent creatures, have done to ourselves and our natural life systems.

Somehow, we have become hypnotised into believing that we are not really interdependent with the natural world. Unintentional trance-based learning has shaped many belief systems from religion to consumerism. For example, we often learn from our major religions that we are superior to other life on Earth and we learn from our economic systems that only humans have intrinsic value, with everything else only having utilitarian value for our purposes.

However, what has been our downfall can also be our salvation. Indigenous people have always used the skill of trance-based learning to assure that perceived authority figures never took control of their beliefs and to optimise ways of achieving that which they wanted to manifest. They well understood the power of learning while in intentional or spontaneous alternative states of consciousness and also had the discipline, focus and techniques for staying on the red road. We can do the same.

This use of trance phenomenon for learning and acting according to what is real and true may be the missing link for bringing us into integrity with our evolved nature. I contend that the hegemonic manipulations of the ruling elite, and the media and textbooks under their control, relate to the phenomenon of spontaneous hypnosis. This phenomenon occurs especially during times of stress when the language coming from a perceived trusted authority figure make us hyper-suggestible to their carefully worded, persuasive mandates.

Hypnotic learning during alternative states of consciousness and alternate brainwave experience is a part of Nature's survival repertoire for a number of animals besides humans. However, we have not been taught about this natural tool. Indeed, the idea of hypnosis has largely been relegated to stage hypnosis, Hollywood, or even the devil. And when we do respect the concept, we pay high fees for professional hypnotherapists, and it is often a last ditch effort toward personal healing. As a result, we have lost our own *intentional* hypnotic skills and have given control of the phenomenon to our preachers, peddlers and politicians – or any other person we have allowed to have some authority over us.

And yet the actual practice of self-hypnosis is easy. Although we can use repetitive chanting, dancing, vision quests, and other traditional methods, simply using a pendulum on a string held between your finger and thumb and imagining it going around in a circle can shift brain wave frequencies into a light trance. The ideomotor neurons fire in the fingers with enough force to move the pendulum. This works when we shift out of beta brain waves sufficiently for a positively-phrased directive to be brought into one's psyche, as in clinical or spontaneous hypnosis. The results seem magical, as does the movement of the pendulum. Of course, this takes some practise. The trick is keeping the pendulum circling, while simultaneously imaging the directive. One can learn self-hypnosis in many ways, and I have described it in a chapter of my book, *Point of Departure*.[67]

Such intentional self-hypnotic skills also include the ability to 'believe in images' via self-induction into appropriate altered states of awareness. You can still give explicit permission to others, such as healers or specialised wisdom keepers, or professionals to induce trances and to implant words for you and help you formulate them. Ultimately, however, all hypnosis is self-hypnosis and is based on the images that words create. Words have always been understood as sacred vibrational frequencies. They are, as Kipling said, mankind's most potent drug.[68] Even Freud, who against the wishes of his friend, Jung, refused to use hypnosis, said that, "Words were originally magic and to this day words have retained much of their ancient magical power."[69]

According to Indigenous wisdom, words also have to be used with truth-seeking in mind. In his text, *A Time Before Deception*,[70] Thomas Cooper offers a scholarly study of how words were seen as sacred to American Indians. They understood words as being about describing reality, and thought that people who lied had a mental illness in which they could not judge truth from falsity. One might consider this to be an explanation for the behaviour we see today that largely ignores the essential priorities of the *chanku luta*, including:

> *Wo'wicake Ocowasiŋ*, All truth.
> *Wo'takuye Ocowasiŋ*, All relatives.
> *Wo'waŝtedake Ocowasiŋ*, All love.
> *Wo'okiye Ocowasiŋ*, All peace.
> *Wo'ksape Ocowasiŋ*, All wisdom.

STANDING ROCK AS A RETURN TO INDIGENOUS CONSCIOUSNESS

I close with some references to my three 'tours of duty' at Standing Rock in North Dakota where Indigenous people from around the world joined with non-Indians from every walk of life and spiritual tradition to protect the sacred waters (*mni wiconi*) of the Missouri River and all who depend on it. What happened at Standing Rock was guided by a sense of *wolokolkiciapi*. Even after the most ruthless attacks by state police trained by corporate-hired mercenaries, the water protectors maintained their loving, prayerful and contagious peacefulness within and without. They have always (or mostly) spoken with authentic love to their 'brothers' in riot gear, in spite of the police officers' snarling faces and threatening words. At worst, the protectors lectured the police as being 'misguided by the priority of a pay check'. They told them to their faces and in the throes of military violence that they are not 'bad people'. The protectors prayed for the police, even while being pepper sprayed, or shot at with rubber bullets.

Throughout the weeks I spent there, whether on an action or in camp, commentary from the water protectors, the Indians and non-Indians alike, reflected a love of the land and the creatures of it, especially of a love of the mighty Missouri River itself which they were there to protect. The Standing Rock movement is, indeed, one that is full of a love that flows like the river, a love that can only flourish when we truly *love* the flow of the river itself as being part of the flow of our own blood and with the same essence.

Standing Rock, and what it accomplished initially, in finally getting the Army to require Energy Transfer Partners to get the Environmental Impact Statement they had managed to avoid previously, might be a model for us all, even if the administration order is now somehow reversed. The process has initiated an awakening of consciousness around the world. Like many other Indigenous-led movements to protect land and water around the globe, it reveals the power of *wolokolkiciapi* and its relationship to prayerful ceremony. It shows how complementarity and alternative consciousness work together, with love and compassion to seek and take responsibility for what is truthful. Those who have worked with the many First Nations people at Standing Rock have learned a very different way of communicating, a way that emphasises interconnectedness with many other-than or greater-than human entities.

This is beautifully expressed by the words of my friend and a fellow member of Veterans for Peace, Tarak Kauff, with which I close this chapter. They are from his interview by Dennis Trainer, Jr., the producer of Acronym TV.[71]

DENNIS: So, why are you here?

TARAK: Well, this is the third time I've been to Standing Rock. The reason I'm here? I guess there's multiple reasons. I feel what is going on here is so important nationally and internationally. It's not just about the water. It's not just about the pipeline. But it is about the sovereignty of the Indian nations. This is really important. As a member of Veterans for Peace, we have a commitment to stop war, all wars. This war has been going on for 500 years! And it is a genocidal war. And don't forget that the armed forces participated in the genocide. We are all part of it, that genocide, and we need to make up for it.

This pipeline and the disregard for sacred native land and for the water is part of that war. And I saw it as such. I mean, this is warfare right here in America. And the people are standing up to it. It is a heroic stand and community is coming together. It's a great manifestation of community that transcends what happened – what we tried to do in the Occupy Movement. And the reason it transcends that is because these people have roots that go back in-forming community for thousands of years. This wisdom is here. It's a collective consciousness that is absolutely incredible. The first time I came here, I was just amazed that I, as a long-time activist, learned and absorbed from the native leadership here as I have. So I'm here to learn. I'm here to be part of it. I'm here to serve as much as I can as a veteran.

I also see what's happening here, this Indigenous-led, this First Nation thing, as so important because there are people here in America who are still, and who have always been, in touch with the Earth. The Earth is sacred to them. And we – generally white society, white Western society – have lost that sense of sacredness. If we are going to survive as a human species, we need to redevelop that. We need to reawaken that in our consciousness. And here it's awake. It's very, very much awake. They talk about, and to, Mother Earth. They talk about the land, the water. It's a living thing and we need to get that – they've had that for thousands of years. We're relearning it, but it is in all of us. If we are going to survive as a species, we need to remember. They still do, and we are all starting to get it. So, this is a very important reason we are here, maybe transcending anything else that's going on.

DENNIS: What does victory look like?

TARAK: I think there has already been a victory here. Over 200 Indigenous tribes have come together that have not been together for hundreds of years. White people, black people, brown people – have all come together in solidarity. That's a victory, and the whole world knows about this. You know, I was in Okinawa with a delegation of veterans standing side by side with the Okinawan people who are resisting new US bases on their land, because they are also destroying their water and their land, and they knew about Standing Rock. This is months ago! And they were inspired by Standing Rock. People all over the world are standing up to US hegemony and imperialism now, because of the destruction our system has wrought, not only here on native people but all over the world. With 800 bases the US has. And when we saw the police out here! That's a military manifestation. They may as well have been an army. They had all the equipment. And so that's what people are rising up to. We want a peaceful world. We want a sustainable world. We want a world that is without all this violence, and it's all violence.

DENNIS: I love this man. I love this man so much!

TARAK: Likewise.

I end this piece with Tarak's words because I believe they summarise our positive potential for world peace. They reveal how a non-Indian person, one who well knows the horror of war and who has made a lifetime commitment to promoting peace as a representative of the military, fully recognises the legacy of our original wisdom and is even inspired by it. They show that achieving *wolokolkiciapi*, as beautiful a concept as it is, requires that we all dig deep into courage and fearlessness. Such traits will not only be required to stand non-violently before those who mock peace, but also to reclaim a worldview that guided us for most of our history on Mother Earth.

54. Four Arrows, Jacobs, J. & Ryan, S., March 15, 2010, 'Anthropocentrism's Antidote: Reclaiming Our Indigenous Orientation to Non-Human Teachers', *Critical Education*, Vol. 1, No.3, Vancouver, CA.: University of British Columbia.

55. Four Arrows, 2008, *Unlearning the Language of Conquest*, Austin: University of Texas Press.

56. Four Arrows, 2014, *The Continuing Saga of Anti-Indianism in America: Critique of a Bestseller and Reviewers Who Praise It*, Truthout.

57. J Dennen, 2005, 'The Origins of War: The Politics of Peace (and War) in Preliterate Societies', *Default Journal*, No. 1.

58. G Leavitt, 1977, 'The Frequency of Warfare: An Evolutionary Perspective', in *Sociological Inquiry*, 47, 49-58.

59. L T Hobhouse, G Wheeler, and M Ginsberg, 1915, *The Material Culture and Social Institutions of the Simpler Peoples*, London: London School of Economics, Monogram.

60. L T Hobhouse, 1956, 'The Simplest Peoples. Part II: Peace and Order Among the Simplest', *The British Journal of Sociology*, 96-119.

61. E Kals, D Schumacher, and L Montada, 1999, 'Emotional affinity towards nature as a motivational basis to protect nature', *Environment & Behaviour*, 31 (2), 178-202.

62. G Cajete, 2000, *Native Science: Natural Laws of Interdependnence*, New Mexico: Clear Light Publishers, 184.

63. Ibid, 186.

64. Personal communication with the author.

65. C G Jung, 1966, 'The Practice of Psychotherapy: Essays on the Psychology of the Transference and Other Subjects', *Collected Works, Volume 16*, New Jersey: Princeton University Press, Vol. 7, para. 327.

66. P Shepard, Edited by Max Oelschlaeger, 1992, 'A Post-Historic Primitivism', *The Wilderness Condition: Essays on Environment and Civilization*, Washington DC: Island Press, 47.

67. Four Arrows teaches this practice in a chapter of his book, *Point of Departure: Returning to*

Our More Authentic Worldview for Education and Survival, 2015.

68. His full quote, from a speech he made to the Royal College of Surgeons in 1923 is, "Words are, of course, the most powerful drug used by mankind. Not only do words infect, egotize, narcotize, and paralyze, but they enter into and colour the minutest cells of the brain [...]" (See http://www.integrativelongevity.org/blog/words-are-powerful-drugs)

69. S Freud, Edited and translated by J Stacey, 1915-1917, 'The Complete Introductory Lectures on Psychoanalysis', *The Standard Edition of the Complete Psychological Works of Sigmund Freud*, Volumes 15 and 16, New York, Norton, 17.

70. T Cooper, 1998, *A Time Before Deception*, New Mexico: Clear Light Publisher, 3.

71. The interview can be seen on YouTube, where the emotions and the love come through better than words on a page: youtube.com/watch?v=UI_2GYdXka8

PART II

PART II

PEACEFULNESS IN THE COMMUNITIES

INTRODUCTION

THE SECOND PART OF THE book explores community as a bridge between our inner peacefulness and the apparent absence of peace 'out there' in the world. In attempting to understand what community is and how people live together in the community, the contributors bring the notion of 'right relationships' into sharper focus. They maintain that peace is ultimately relational, and that right relationships include not only the relation that a person has with his/her self, and our relations with one another, amongst social groups and communities, but also apply at the institutional and structural/systemic level. Additionally, they are further applicable to the relations that a person or a group has with their past, present and future.

This relational view of peace distinguishes itself from other conceptions in two major ways: the first is that peace cannot just be a thing 'out there', attainable through reducing and eliminating violence and warfare. Instead, relational peace suggests that peace resides in our everyday realities and communities, and it is created and recreated in our myriad forms of relating. Furthermore, peace is not necessarily an end state, but rather it is an ongoing and intentional process, and our endeavour to make peace is closely connected to our 'being peace' with each other, that is, proactively living out the peacefulness inspired by our spiritual way of being. As our contributors point out, peace in the world is not limited to the charge of politicians and international organisations, although their part to construct the conditions for peacefulness to flourish is critical – peace is, indeed, everyone's responsibility.

In Chapter Four, Scherto Gill, a Research Fellow at the Guerrand-Hermès Foundation for Peace and the University of Sussex, seeks to understand what community is and focuses her discussion on those conceptions that stress the relational nature of our being and social transformation. She argues that *being is communing*, a radical form of being-with, a co-presence or inter-being, which finds its source in the mystery of being human. Our commitment to deep relatedness creates the promise of peace in the world.

Following on, in Chapter Five, philosopher and theologian, Joseph Milne of the Temenos Academy and the Eckhart Society, discusses peacefulness within the philosophical and theological propositions of the pre-Enlightenment, a period which saw the cosmos as ordered, harmonious and whole.

This harmony and wholeness determine that, instead of self-sovereignty and the social contract, our openness to transcendence and the cosmic law would draw all beings towards their full fulfilment in true community.

These two chapters set a solid conceptual basis for Chapter Six where Marianne Marstrand, director of the Global Peace Initiative of Women (GPIW), discusses how spiritual peace manifested through feminine wisdom is proactively lived in the world, rather than laissez-faire. In particular, she offers a number of grounded and moving stories of GPIW's activities as beautiful illustrations to show how wholeness and harmony can be restored in communities, including war-torn ones, by the power of love and of communing.

Conceiving peace and peacefulness from such relational perspectives will enable us to see conflicts and tensions as necessary elements of peacefulness. They invite dialogue, listening and creative imagination and demand faith in humanity.

CHAPTER **FOUR**

UNDERSTANDING COMMUNITY AS COMMUNING

SCHERTO GILL

IN THIS CHAPTER, I EXPLORE a different way of understanding community – community as communing and focus the discussion on those conceptions of community that stress the relational nature of our being. I argue that this relational way of being is *being-with* which finds its source in the mystery of being human, in our intersubjectivity.[72] This is where peacefulness lies and where being peace begins and making peace in the world becomes possible. Embedded in the conception of peace in this book is an active and even proactive form of relating which rejects a static and passive way of being in the world. Indeed, as I shall illustrate through the different ingredients of communing, our relational way of being peace is the basis of political activism, cultural innovation and social transformation towards a betterment of humanity.

To deepen our understanding of community as communing, this chapter first investigates such questions as: 'How do we understand our being as being-with?'; 'What does it mean to be in a community through being-with?' and 'How will being-with each other and being-with the ultimate or divine Other change our being-with the world?' It then proposes a set of key aspirations that not only illustrate how we might commune with all that is, but also keep alive the idea of the wholeness of being, at the heart of which lies the flourishing of all (that is, humankind, other beings and the planet), including the flourishing of our relationships. Finally, by reflecting on how these different values can be creatively nurtured, pursued and lived in the day-to-day lives of people, this chapter highlights the salient connection between relationships, dialogue and peace in the world.

UNDERSTANDING COMMUNITY AS COMMUNING

There has been an overall assumption that community is good and desirable, if not an imperative to our way of being together. Sociologists, philosophers, psychologists, peace researchers and educationalists are amongst those who have promoted the notion of community. The idea of global community is even more inspiring as a vision of peace and harmony amongst the diverse people on the planet. Although there is not an ultimate definition of community, there are, however, compelling and convergent ideas emerging from the different conceptions of community. Amongst them is the proposal that our being is fundamentally relational, that community reflects the social and interdependent nature of our being. In this sense, our being is always already 'being-with'. The word 'with' really captures the essence of our being – a genuine *coesse*, (co-being, or being-with), a mutual presence or co-presence, which is found in love, trust and respect for each other.

For the purposes of our discussion, we distinguish three kinds of being-with: (1) being-with others; (2) being-with the divine Other; (3) being-with the world, including the social and natural world. I will now turn to each separately and then will later bring them together to discuss community as communing.

BEING-WITH OTHERS: Human life is simultaneously material, emotional, intellectual, social, moral and spiritual and comprises diverse experiences, activities and processes. As life itself has intrinsic value, then so does the person who is living such a life. This points to the moral nature of being human, central to which is an acceptance of other people as moral beings who are equally worthy of our love and respect, however different they may be from ourselves.

At the same time, being human involves being aware that we are finite, and our ways of being, our practices and worldviews are always situated in our histories, memories, collective wounds, religious teachings, cultural traditions and communal journeys. So it is imperative for us to engage with others and their otherness, and to be in relationship with others in order to overcome our limitedness and to transcend the human condition.[73] In this way, our growth is not only enriched by those others we encounter, but it is also codependent on the growth of others and the development of humanity as a whole.[74]

This inherently relational way of being human challenges the predominant Western individualism, a mentality which tends to put 'me' first, and gives priority to the individual's self-interest, self-perfection and self-actualisation. What is favoured in the individualistic orientation is competitiveness, dominance, control, fear of others and fear of difference, hence the resulting separation, alienation and annihilation, as well as the constant risk and threat of violence. People, groups and society will experience a lack of peacefulness whenever there is too much self-absorption and self-obsession. Where relationships are encouraged, and even at all possible, they are largely instrumental, aimed at serving a goal for individual pursuit or success. This also means that relationships are part of the cost-effect calculation: "How much time and money will it cost me to develop a relationship with X? And what will X offer me in return?"

By contrast, the relational vision of one's self is not situated in a static way of being, instead, it is the locus of 'all intelligible action.'[75] Thus, peace depends on the care devoted to relationships and relational processes. In this way, the self should never be understood as a singular bounded individual, but instead, each person experiences him or herself as a relational being, the meaningfulness of whose existence is intimately connected to that of others.[76]

When understanding our way of being from such a relational perspective, we can see that the person is a *participating* subject whose being and acting is achieved through relationships with others and our co-presence in the world, an illustration of being-with.[77] The notion of a participating subject implies that as a person, we view ourselves as a being *among* beings. This affirms that each of us is an end in him or herself, rather than an object in the world. Here participation involves the presence of one's self with other persons, other beings, and with the world. Gabriel Marcel calls this *disponibilité*, or availing. This is achieved when we are communing with others, in an interdependent and mutually constitutive relationship.

This leads us to suggest a further point that each person is also a *contributing* subject, where we view ourselves as a being *for* other beings, whose relationship with others is realised through a form of care, respect, and deep concern for others in the world. This caring can also be directed at one's self. As Parker Palmer points out, our self is the only gift we can offer to others, and whenever we listen to our self and give it the care it needs, we are at the same time caring for others.[78] We contribute through our being and availing ourselves to others, through our growth and development, our synergetic relationship with others, and through our service to others and to the world at large.

Other thinkers have characterised this way of being-with as the *fellowship* of men and women. For instance, Scottish philosopher, John Macmurray, draws our attention to the irreducible importance of the other in our own life and in our own being, stressing the intersubjective nature of trans- cendent human conditions.[79] He maintains that the presence of the other is imperative in our own being a person and claims that there can be no person whatsoever, without two persons in relation. Macmurray suggests that to be in relationship with someone, such as to love another person, means that we are aware of the other "more and more completely and delicately". This relationship is not instrumental or what he calls functional, instead, it defines the natural way that we take delight in the other's exist- ence for its own sake. Being-with others, according to Macmurray, is the only way of being human.

We can further elucidate this ethical nature of being-with by using Martin Buber's exploration of an 'I-thou' relationship.[80] According to Buber, we humans possess a two-fold attitude towards the world: the 'I-Thou' and the 'I-It.' The 'I-Thou' relationship stresses the mutual and holistic exist- ence of two entities. It is an encounter of equals who recognise each other as such. The 'I-Thou' relationship contains a dialogue. By contrast, the 'I-It' relationship emphasises the other being as an object to be used or instrumentalised, and experienced as a means to an end, failing to recog- nise the other as an equal or of having equal worth to oneself. The 'I-It' relationship contains no dialogue and, instead, it involves distancing where the division between the two is accentuated and the uniqueness of 'I' stressed. As a result, the 'I' is separated from the self it encounters. The latter is a reflection of the crisis of being in a modern society, as already discussed, where an emphasis on the self makes it more and more difficult for us to encounter the Other, including God or anything divine (see the next section).

So being human is being in communion (in a non-religious sense) with other human beings. This 'I-Thou' relationship determines our being itself to be a form of meeting, communing and dialogue. This brings us back to Marcel's vision that sees each of us as a participating subject. In this sense, our life itself becomes an encounter and dialogue. Likewise, to be in the world as a contributing subject is to collaborate with others in service to goodness for each other and for the world. This two-fold orientation towards self as a pathway to transcendence and transformation in the world reflects the true essence of being-with. So long as we are actively living out our life as human beings, we are already in community, in communing. Communing is action-oriented, which stresses the proactive nature of our being-with.

Thus community is a form of communing where individuals engage in the mutuality of relating and relatedness, as equals. According to Macmurray, being equal has nothing to do with having or possessing things of equivalence, such as equal abilities, equal rights, equal functions or any other kind of de facto equality. This equality means that within a community, no person will treat others as a mere function or a role-occupant. The equality is intentional: it is an aspect of the mutuality of communing and relating. It depicts the essence of love.

BEING-WITH THE DIVINE OTHER: Our being consists in not only the fellowship of men and of women, but also the communing with, or being-with the ultimate or divine Other.

Many religions have expounded that God is the divine being, a true divine Other. God's divine qualities are only realised in their revelation of presence to humans and all that is. In this sense, as persons, we are otherness in communion and communion in otherness, that is, we only exist in relation to the divine 'Thou.'[81] As human beings, our being is defined through relationship with the divine Other and, without such relationship, we lose this precious otherness, the 'Thou,' in ourselves and in the divine. To be is to seek, to remain and to sustain this relationship. Affirming the divine through our communion with God is to affirm our own being. In this sense, without communion with the divine Other, it would be impossible to speak of being. By being-with the divine Other, we aspire for God's way of being. In other words, God is not an entity to be merely 'believed in' – instead, God is the divine Other that human beings 'live with' and with whom true dialogue and encounter is necessary. Macmurray proposes that religions no longer guard a vision of the divine –religion's purpose is to sustain the intention to achieve such communion with the divine.

Marcel calls the ultimate Other an 'Absolute Thou', which is not limited to God. Absolute Thou is an absolute Presence, seen in a de-sacralised way that doesn't require any confessional faith. In Buber's terms, this is the eternal Thou.[82] Each and every 'I-Thou' relationship opens up a window to the ultimate Thou or the divine Other.

Indeed, many non-confessional wisdom traditions provide a different insight and maintain that the divine quality is not limited to God's being, but is also found in all animate beings in the world. So there is divine Nature in animals, trees, and in other beings. Indeed, most indigenous traditions have always maintained that Nature itself is divine. In modern living, many indigenous worldviews have been rediscovered and re-accepted as long-lost truths to combat the instrumentalisation of both human lives and the planet's natural resources. Recognising the divine nature of all beings is to affirm the oneness of all life, and, likewise, to consolidate each person's place in relation to other human beings, and our communities, as well as our community's place in our immediate and more distant environment, and, furthermore, in all that is within the wider system or universe. In this sense, being with the divine other is a true celebration of communion, a celebration and appreciation of the fellowship amongst all things sacred.

BEING-WITH THE WORLD: Macmurray suggests that the life of community is to be a fellowship of the world – man with man, and man with the world, including nature.[83] Freire elucidates this point further by rejecting any suggestion implicit or explicit that 'man is abstract, isolated, independent, and unattached to the world', or that 'the world exists as a reality apart from people.'[84] Echoing Macmurray, Freire evokes that being a person is living out our human qualities in the world with a view to changing it. There is an interconnectedness between persons and the world, according to Freire – hence, it is not persons in the world, but rather persons with others and with the world, representing a constant striving for the emergence of consciousness and a critical intervention with reality.

Likewise, a Gadamerian view of community stresses our being-with each other as being in the world, a Heideggerian *Dasien*, or being. Being-with demands openness to ongoing revision of our own prejudice, instilling the necessity to engage in continued self-cultivation and self-transcendence. Being in a community itself is a form of dialogue and dialogue is our being-in-the-world. Gadamer argues that we do not enter into dialogue, instead, we find ourselves already in dialogue – but only IF we are listening intensely and deeply and engaging with the other and with the world.[85]

Being a person involves becoming consciously aware of our existence in the world with which and in which we find ourselves. Thus community is not only constituted through human fellowship and solidarity, but also provides a context within which each individual proactively pursues being-with each other in the world and with the world, and through this communing, we transform the world and human lives within it. This way of understanding communing offers an understanding of the nature of work – work is no longer just a means to make a livelihood, but it is an expression of who we are, and it enriches the community's life, strengthens human fellowship and serves the goodness in the world.

SUMMARY

In this part of the discussion, we explored community as communing from three perspectives: communing as being-with each other, as being-with the divine Other and as being-with the world. These three kinds of being-with suggest that the meaning of our being lies in the web of relationships we engage in, and the value of community rests precisely on the quality of these relations. That is also to say that community is not a framework or container within which individuals are helped by others to pursue their personal interests. Community is not a means – instead, it is a way of being formed by being-with or communing.

Community embodies solidarity amongst people and, as we have seen, solidarity rejects the commonalities or shared interests which would render it superficial. Instead, being historically and culturally situated, people bond with one another as the other. Thus community is a dialogue and an unfolding mutual inquiry.[86] In such communities, dialogue partners are co-investigators in whose inquiry, there lies the imperative to disclose the roots of modern social malaises, such as violent conflict, exploitation of the planet Earth, inequality and so on. This includes critical self-awareness of transforming any possible hindrances within one's own tradition and culture that might impede a social movement towards a peaceful and flourishing world.

PEACE THROUGH COMMUNING –
SEVEN KEY FEATURES

This inquiry has led us to investigate and propose a set of key ingredients and features that not only define and characterise community, but also help keep alive in community the common end of the flourishing of all, including the flourishing of relationships. This, as we shall argue, counts as a key to peace.

FRIENDSHIP AND FELLOWSHIP: We have established that to be a person is to be in relationship with other people. This relationship has been characterised by Macmurray as personal, as opposed to functional, because the primacy of relationship is a fundamental aspect of human life. He goes as far as claiming that, "We need one another to be ourselves," highlighting our intention of prioritising the relational way of our being.[87] Therefore, this intention to be-with marks the first feature of community – the friendship and fellowship between people.

In friendship and fellowship, we can find true freedom to be fully ourselves as we are no longer hindered by fear (of others, judgement, and mistakes) or suspicion. This is because what underlies friendship and fellowship is love, acceptance and an appreciation of the other as part of our own well-being and flourishing (also, see 'We-ness' below), and hence mutual concern and genuine care for each other. In this sense, when we are in community, we are in fellowship – fellowship of men/women and fellowship of the world – with our planet and all beings on Earth. This relational way of being extends human peacefulness to the realm of Nature, so that peace and peacefulness are bound up with our relationship with each other and with the natural world.

WE-NESS: In communities, the ways in which we connect to other people is by thinking, feeling and perceiving ourselves and the other not as 'me and you', but as 'us'. In this way, our relationship with others becomes a part/whole relation. In other words, we become part of each other's lives and their meaning through this 'we'-awareness, or 'we'-consciousness.

For each one of the 'we', the other is part of one's life. Furthermore, he argues that 'we'-consciousness is self-reflective – each person can recognise that they regard themselves and each other as 'we' or 'us.' Accordingly, suggests Thomson, this self-reflective 'we'-awareness can transform the bonds between people from the interpersonal (as a relation among persons) to the collective intrapersonal (as a relation between members of a group). Such bonds can further enable communal activity, or people doing things together as a group. We-ness contains in itself a way of being or acting that is communal, where personal aims are essentially collective – that is, ours. We will return to the idea of collective intentionality, a connected idea, later.

PRESENCE: To be communing means to be receptive to the call of others as a presence. Marcel describes this as *disponibilité*, an active, more developed sense of availability to others.[88] Presence as availing is not passive; rather, it is actively seeking out relationships with others, and being actively engaged in concern for others.

This is contrast to non-presence, a passivity which results in fear, hesitancy and powerlessness, the presence of one person can transform the life and experience of another in a constructive sense – so by immersing ourselves in the being of others and availing ourselves to others, we experience the wholeness of being.

Presence invites participating subjects and it can only be invoked or evoked in availing and encountering. Presence, through communing and availing, enables a person to come into a complete participation with another being. For Marcel, it means that the self is 'given' to the other, and that 'given-ness' is responsively received or reciprocated. (The reciprocity of presence is a necessary condition for it.) Where presence is mutual, it denotes our openness to each other. At the same time, presence is non-linguistic and, therefore, it is a true communing, an enveloping of each other's being, and, above all, a real encounter of beings. Where one avails oneself to others, one is equally more present towards the self. In other words, communing with others can give new meaning to experiences that otherwise would have been closed to the self.

Peace entails that we become a community of beings, all of whom are committed to the same end, which is the next feature of communing.

COLLECTIVE INTENTION: Community is sustained by the intention of communing. According to Searle,[89] collective intention is where people share intentional states, such as beliefs, desires and intentions. Football games, orchestras, social activism, and building a house together, are all examples of activities that involve collective intentionality. Collective intentionality reflects the content of people's desires, wants, and beliefs, directed at something in the world (in our discussion, the collective intention of community is peace and peacefulness).

However, collective intention differs from the notion of group mind. When it is common striving or general will, collective intention is not dependent on an individual's personal interests, nor is it the sum of private wills. Thus, it is we-intention rather than I-intention, and collective intention is irreducibly collective. Any individual acts can be, in part, a collectively coordinated purposeful act, such as the way individual instrumentalists in the orchestra play a symphony together.

Collective intention is also conceived as practical social consciousness (as in 'we will do something together').[90] Within a society, individuals can have a general idea of the social or moral enterprise as a whole to which they commit themselves. Equally, each individual is convinced that there are other people who are partners with them in this common endeavour, without having to know who exactly they are. So, a community, or even a society, has no other will than the will of its members; no other activity, but the activity of its members; no other responsibility, but the responsibility of its members. In this way, communal activities or doing things together as a collective endeavour towards something that is most desirable for all, such as peace, is not only possible, but it is also in our fundamental interests and wellbeing to do so.

DIALOGUE: Buber establishes that dialogue is located in the in-between space of the I and Thou. Genuine dialogue is the meeting of souls because the I-Thou encounter can only take place between whole beings, including our spiritual or higher self. The life of dialogue involves 'the turning towards the other', not by seeking, but by grace, as if we are called to dialogue.

For Buber, 'attentive silence' is the basis of dialogue.[91] Silence is active, and is regarded as a welcoming acceptance of the other, a deeper sense of knowing, and any word born out of silence is received in silence. In silence arises the stillness, which is located in the aforementioned in-between space, a generative space.

Similarly, listening in dialogue is a form of love and acceptance and we listen in ways that both hold our perceptions about the other (in order to engage in the dialogue) and lay aside our assumptions about the other (in order for the other to speak to us). It is almost as if we must step outside ourselves, so as to create space for engaging with the other. When the community is a safe space, people are able to venture beyond rhetorical harmony and listen in ways that not only accept, but also seek dissonance, which can build impetus and invite the urge towards resolution, reconciliation, and understanding. Thus, listening involves availing oneself to an other, suspension, silence, inner listening, dwelling, inhabiting within one's own horizon, but also self-transcendence. Deep listening thus requires the receptiveness from the narrator or teller to loving attentiveness (rather than reactiveness) and the give-ness of those who listen and, indeed, deep dialogue embodies an explicit commitment to the equal value of the realities of all persons.

AUTHORSHIP: In the context of a Western obsession with the self and an overwhelming zest for portraying the individualised ego, and with the burgeoning domination of narrative therapy and autobiographies in search of the self and other storied self-centrality and preoccupations with the individual, the narrative of community is a refreshing way to strengthen we-ness, celebrate myriad traditions, and co-construct meanings in our being-with and being together. In fact, there is only one way to see the perpetuation of community – that is, through an ongoing authorship that tells the story of communing, which is a necessary response to the cultural, socio-economic and political change that results in the alienation of people from each other. In other words, we are co-creating our communities through stories. Thus, it is necessary to reflect on the various elements that comprise authorial voice(s) and the responsibility each person assumes in the process of authoring.

A key ingredient in authoring the narrative of community is its non-linear approach to the process of storying our communing. This authoring is around the day-to-day dialogue, listening and enquiring into the collective life of what it means to be in communion. Hence, authorship also carries within itself the important task of developing the language of community, the language of being-with, the language born out of a set of relationships unique to each community of being-with, and the language that is the fruit of coordinated action.[92]

Another core ingredient is that the narrative of community is always subject to conflicting and multiple interpretations of the past, be that a community of intention or the community of memory. As each narrative and interpretation of the past is aimed at offering a particular understanding of the present, when putting stories together, they become crucial in the ongoing dialogue about what is to come in terms of a collective future.

The centrality of listening, in particular, deep listening, is found in the process of authoring, which attends to both voices and silences, and endorses perspectives derived from different traditions and weaves in conflicting discourses, whilst, all the while, co-authoring a new tradition, co-creating a living culture of communing. No wonder Macmurray writes, "Only in a community can a living culture be developed."[93]

A further element in authoring is myth-making. Myths, which exist in our collective imagination as religious myths, national myths, and legal myths, all consist in the narratives people have told about the values, hopes and aspirations that a community has wished to live by. In making myth, we are tuning in to rich languages and discourses, articulating what is worthwhile in human life, and it is under this horizon that we, as a community of people, must take a stand and pursue our collective intention together. In this way, we are not just creating a myth for a community to follow, we are not only authoring our selves, but we are equally authoring the world.[94] In this way, narrative-making and myth-making in a community becomes world-making.

TRANSCENDENCE: Transcendence is typically understood to be something that 'goes beyond'. However, Marcel insists that transcendence is reaching towards a height, a trans-ascendance, to 'strive towards an increasingly pure mode of experience.' It is not, however, transcending experience – instead, it is having an experience of the transcendent.[95] According to Marcel, this way of understanding the transcendent does not necessarily mean that it is fully comprehensible, but, nevertheless, it is something that we attend to and care about. As Marcel writes:

> There is an order where the subject finds himself in the presence of something entirely beyond his grasp. I would add that if the word 'transcendent' has any meaning it is here — it designates the absolute, unbridgeable chasm yawning between the subject and being, insofar as being evades every attempt to pin it down.[96]

It is also implicit in Marcel's writing that transcendence involves a radical love, which is not only present in the unconditional, but also in the sign of presence and availing, a presence embodied in the 'us.' Community as communing is a celebration of communion with all that is – a fellowship of things in the cosmos. This meeting with and living with the divine Other is obviously dynamic and full of movement. Such meeting is never a mere religious practice, or a ritual – instead, it is always located in the concrete struggle and striving of the community. Indeed, as Parker Palmer suggests, a true community will necessarily require a transcendent third thing that holds each person accountable to something beyond ourselves. The transcendent dimension of community is hence not detached from what we say and do.[97]

PEACE THROUGH COMMUNING

In this chapter, I have made an attempt to understand community and have alluded to the notion of community as being-with or communing. Adopting this relationally-focused way of conceiving community does not reduce the complexities involved in the concept, instead it invites more dialogue to bring about the richness of other ways of understanding community.

Community as communing is more than a philosophical articulation, although I have drawn heavily on several philosophers' thoughts and views. This conception is not unique and it is intimately connected to the notion of peace put forward by the Earth Charter, which says that, "Peace is the wholeness created by right relationships with oneself, other persons, other cultures, other life, Earth, and the larger whole of which all are a part."[98] The two key concepts here are wholeness and right relationships. Peace, when so defined, is communing with all that is.

The real significance of this way of understanding community lies in its potential to serve as a form of praxis, that is to say, an indication of how we can relate to things and actions in the world and ground our relationships in the different kinds of being-with. This is essentially a pathway to peacefulness. It simultaneously stresses both the rich relational contents of being-with and the action-oriented aspiration of being-with. Indeed, the implications of the verb 'communing' could not be more explicit – it emphasises those ways of living and flourishing already mentioned, including, for instance, encountering, dialogue, listening, co-authoring and co-acting. Here, community is not an end in itself, but rather communing as a way of being in the world is a gift that we offer to, and receive from, each other reciprocally.

However, to live out this gift for one another and move towards peace in the world does not always come naturally or easily because in our personal, socio-economic and political lives, as well as our cultural practice, we must cultivate in each person the capacity and responsibility for relating and connectedness.

We can see now that to instil a culture of peace through communing and human relatedness might require at least four interlocking ways of nurturing peacefulness.

The first is the personal endeavour of putting in some deep *inner* work which would be centred around living a contemplative life. Our innate longing for peacefulness can only be realised through the experience of the transcendent. This inner quietude is achievable by opening ourselves to what is beyond, the transcendent. There are many ways one might pursue a contemplative life, such as through attentive silence, the practice of deep listening, following a particular spiritual path and living mindfully. However, such a spiritual journey of seeking tranquillity and stillness is not an escape from the troubles and torments of the hostile world out there, nor a self-absorbing path of individual development. It is, instead, the basis of mutual presence and true communing.

The second way consists in developing an awareness and appreciation of human relatedness in a flourishing life. Such an endeavour could start from an openness towards experiencing the different ways of being-with in all aspects of our life. Indeed, our opening of ourselves to this transcendent nature of human life can only be cultivated when there is such an intention to move from the 'I' to the 'we', where the 'we', according to the Earth Charter, is inclusive in the broadest sense.

Hence, the third approach to nurture peacefulness involves a political commitment – to create the necessary conditions where the kind of relatedness desirable for our communing can flourish. This political commitment requires an intentional effort to also explore the relationships of large groups – the relationships between communities, and our relationship with our collective past. The latter is particularly relevant to societies that have once been torn apart by wars and violent conflict. This would also encourage societies to start promoting harmonious relationships between formerly divided communities as the basis for conflict transformation and post-conflict peacebuilding.

The last and most fundamental way of fostering our capacities for communing is through education, so that people's deepest needs for friendship and fellowship, and people's awareness of themselves as a participating and contributing subject, are cultivated at an early age. This includes developing safe and humanising educational environments where relationships can flourish, and where there is a culture of listening, dialogue, and caring.

In the same vein, curriculum activities and pedagogical and evaluative practices are to be situated within relational processes, so that any form of alienation and separation is not possible. In other words, schools are not just places where children and young people learn about relationships; but rather they learn in relationships.

Globally, for the first time, humanity has come ever so close to living together in ONE community on the planet Earth. So long as we see love as the promise of belonging, community as the commitment to our deep relatedness, and the human spirit as an experience of transcendence, such global community will be possible.

---

72. Gabriel Marcel, Translated by G S Fraser, 1951, *The Mystery of Being, Vol.1, Reflection and Mystery*, London: The Harvill Press.

73. Gadamer, 1969, *Truth and Method,* London: Bloomsbury.

74. Gadamer, 1976, *Philosophical Hermeneutics*; Freire, 1970, *Pedagogy of the Oppressed*; Macmurray, 1961.

75. K Gergen, 2011, *Relational Being*, New York: Oxford University Press, 281.

76. K J Gergen, 1991, *The Saturated Self: Dilemmas of Identity in Contemporary Life*, New York: Basic Books.

77. G Marcel, 1951, *The Mystery of Being.* Great Britain: The Harvill Press Ltd.

78. P J Palmer, 1993, *Let Your Life Speak,* San Francisco, Jossey-Bass.

79. J Macmurray, J, 1961, *Reason and Emotion*, New York: Faber and Faber.

80. M Buber, Translated by R G Smith, 1958, *I and Thou*, Edinburgh, T&T. Clark and M Buber, Translated by R G Smith, 1947, *Between Man and Man*, London: Kegan Paul.

81. J Zizoulas, 1985, *Being as Communion: Studies in Personhood and the Church,* London: DLT.

82. M Buber, Translated by R G Smith, 1958, *I and Thou*, Edinburgh: T & T Clark, 99.

83. J Macmurray, 1961.

84. P Freire, 1970, *Pedagogy of the Oppressed*, New York: Herder and Herder.

85. H G Gadamer, 1969, *Truth and Method*, London: Bloomsbury.

86. H G Gadamer, 1976, *Philosophical Hermeneutics,* Berkeley: University of California Press.

87. J Macmurray, 1961, 211.

88. G Marcel, Translated by G S Fraser, 1951a, *The Mystery of Being, Vol. 1, Reflection and Mystery*, London: The Harvill Press; G Marcel, Translated by René Hague, 1951b, *The Mystery of Being, Vol. 2, Faith and Reality,* London: The Harvill Press.

89. J R Searle, 1995, *Construction of Social Reality*, New York: The Free Press.

90. See, for instance, R G Collingwood, 1947, *The Idea of Nature*, England: Clarendon.

91. D Avnon, 1998, *Martin Buber: The Hidden Dialogue (20th Century Political Thinkers)*, Colorado: Rowman & Littlefield, 42-3.

92. K J Gergen, 2009, *Relational Being: Beyond Self and Community*, New York: Oxford University Press.

93. J Macmurray,,1968, *Freedom in the Modern World*, New York: Faber & Faber, 35.

94. J Macmurray, 1961, 165.

95. G Marcel, 1951, *The Mystery of Being*, Great Britain: The Harvill Press Ltd, 39.

96. G Marcel, Translated by Stephen Jolin and Peter McCormick, Edited by John Wild, 1973, *Tragic Wisdom and Beyond*, Evanston: Northwestern University Press, 193.

97. P Palmer, 1977, *A Place called Community*, Pennsylvania: Pendle Hill Publications.

98. Earth Charter, http://earthcharter.org/discover/the-earth-charter/

CHAPTER **FIVE**

PEACE AND OUR FORGOTTEN CITIZENSHIP

JOSEPH MILNE

One must also consider in which of the two ways the
nature of the whole contains what is good and what is best,
whether as something separate, itself by itself, or as the
order of the whole of things.

Aristotle, *Metaphysics*, 1075a

PHILOSOPHY, POETRY, RELIGION, AND MYTH all began in the human sense of cosmic harmony. Human consciousness itself is rooted in a primordial intuition of this harmony, and so the human soul finds itself placed within this vast, complex, mysterious unity. This beginning is experienced by every person who falls still and gazes at the night stars, or upon a horizon of distant mountains, or who listens to the motion of the ocean lapping the shore, or morning birdsong. As Plato says in the *Timaeus*, "Sight is the source of the greatest benefits to us; for if our eyes had never seen the sun, stars, and heavens, the words which we have spoken would not have been uttered."[99]

In abiding in the presence of these mysteries, the soul may come to peace. Yet this peace has within it a call to respond. The universe, Nature, summons the soul to bear witness and give to all things their names and to affirm their goodness of being. This first silence of the soul before all things is the birthplace of thought and speech. They arise in answer to the call from the order of things that they be known and be said to be known. For, even as each human person is made whole in being known, so the universe longs to be known and brought before human reflection for this end.

The birth of thought and speech in reply to the cosmos is, therefore, also the birth of the human species, distinguishing it from all other creatures, for it is Anthropos alone who wonders and enquires into the truth, order, meaning, and goodness of things. But this birth of thought and speech is also the birth of self-reflection and of the mysterious knowledge that the soul must give account of itself before the cosmos. Consciousness and conscience arise together in the human soul. The sense of 'I' and the sense of the 'Whole' come into existence at the same moment, and from this arises the knowledge that the human being must seek to live rightly and wisely and in accord with the harmony of cosmos. Cicero expresses it in this way:

> The primary duty is that the creature should maintain itself in its natural constitution; next, that it should cleave to all that is in harmony with nature and spurn all that is not; and when once this principle of choice and rejection has been arrived at, the next stage is choice, conditioned by inchoate

duty; next such a choice is exercised continuously; finally, it is rendered unwavering and in thorough agreement with nature; and at that stage the conception of what good really is begins to dawn within us and be understood.[100]

Every creature has a duty to maintain its integrity and, while the other creatures do this spontaneously through natural inclination, human nature must take up that obligation voluntarily and deliberately. This is because human nature maintains its natural constitution through aligning itself with the cosmic harmony. So that we may, "cleave to all that is in harmony with nature," as Cicero put it, Plato says in the *Timaeus* that, "God gave us the faculty of sight that we might behold the order of the heavens and create a corresponding order in our own erring minds." The mind is ordered when brought into agreement with the 'order of the heavens', and departs from its own nature when out of agreement with this divine order of things. Knowledge of the heavenly order comes to the mind as a gift from Nature. That is the most ancient experience. The cosmos discloses itself to the soul in four ways: philosophically through understanding, poetically through beauty, mythically through wonder, and religiously through veneration. Each of these four ways are responses to revelation. In their origin, they are utterly innocent.

THE ORIGINAL GOODNESS

So the intuition of humanity in its beginning, in time before time, is of Paradise. This is our original belonging as a people of the Earth. This is an original symbolic knowledge, and we cannot unravel what is expressed symbolically or through the narrative of myth. The original Garden embodies all perfections, all goodness, all abundance, a completeness of life, peace among all creatures, and the true relation between heaven and Earth. This cannot be translated into rational terms because it is a foundational memory in the soul of the primordial condition of things against which the unfolding story of Anthropos moves and takes shape. From that memory, every human being knows they are a sojourner in the world, who one day shall return home to Eden. With this ancient memory also comes the intuition of estrangement, the sense of a lost kingdom. These elements shape all the great myths and sagas of departure and return, from Homer to Tolkien, or from Genesis to Apocalypse.

Plato likewise speaks of the immortal soul descending from the eternal abode of divine truth into the mortal body of material flux, where appearance and truth no longer directly correspond. And so all true knowledge is for Plato anamnesis, recollection of what the soul once beheld directly in eternity. But the embodied soul must learn to distinguish this true knowledge that informs all visible things. Those with the clearest memory are born poets and philosophers, the poet ever seeking beauty, and the philosopher ever seeking wisdom. Yet these callings, although springing from recollection, have within them a yearning and discontent. Like Odysseus, they are driven by the desire to return home. The poet desires to unite with beauty, while the philosopher desires to unite with wisdom. This desire to unite is the ground of love, of Eros. In its longing for unity Eros gives birth to poetry and philosophy, which is to say, the birth of speech or language. "The gifts of speech and hearing were bestowed upon us; not for the sake of irrational pleasure, but in order that we might harmonise the courses of the soul by sympathy with the harmony of sound, and cure ourselves of our irregular and graceless ways," as Plato further explains in the *Timaeus*. Philosophy and poetry are, in a certain sense, healing for the soul, and the philosopher and the poet are also physicians to society.

For the ancients, human society maintains its own nature through being brought into accord with the heavenly order. For Plato, there is a correspondence between the cosmos, the city, and the citizen. The city, the natural human dwelling place, governed by speech, is a small cosmos after the pattern of the great cosmos, and the individual citizen is a small city after the pattern of the great city. For Plato, this means that the *polis* takes form through a combination of correspondences between the divine cosmic order and the order of the soul. In one sense, the polis is a *microcosmos*, and, in another sense, it is a *macroanthropos*, the soul writ large.[101] The polis flourishes in peace when its laws spring from and embody this threefold harmony. Then the citizens love the laws and education, and the arts nurture the natural order of the soul. The opposite condition is where the city splits into factions and is at war with itself, and where chaos threatens to overthrow the natural order. Even now, when this sacred order of society has been largely forgotten and abandoned, the greatest fear is the descent of society into chaos. It then dawns on people that their individuality, which our current age holds in such high regard, is wholly dependent on the common good and lawful order of community, and that the community exists prior to the individual. This was always the ancient understanding. Out of the whole arises each part and each part has its integrity trough living and flourishing in accord with the whole.

NATURAL COMMUNITY

In her remarkable study of Maat, the ancient Egyptian way of life, Maulana Karenga, writes:

> Assman (LA IV, 974) has noted concerning the person in Kemetic society that, "As an individual man is not viable (*lebenfahig*): he lives in and through society." This essentially means that the Maatian community is a communitarian and participatory moral community. Here always the person-in-relationship, i.e., in family, community, society, is the centre of focus as distinct from modern European individualism, in which the individual, abstract, autonomous and often alienated, is the essential focus and center of gravity. In Maatian ethics the sociality of selfhood is defined by roles and relationships and the practice attached to these roles. Self-development becomes a communal act, an act rooted in activity for and of the community. One, then, is not an individual, autonomous and alone, but a person interrelated and encumbered by the relations and demands of one's society.[102]

Maulana further remarks that, "the Maatian society was not simply a human construction, but also a participant in the divine and cosmic ideal and practice of Maat".[103] Again, "humans are embedded in this order with its divine, social and natural aspects. *In their identity as children and images of God, humans belong to the divine; in their identity as social beings, they belong to society; and in their identity as living beings they belong to nature.*"[104]

Belonging to these three realms is to be human. A human being cannot be rightly situated in existence without the sense of belonging to these three realms. This is why Maulana regards the modern notion of selfhood grounded in individual autonomy as alienating. Such alienation must surely account for the many neuroses of modern society. But Plato was alert to this danger as something that must be given consideration in creating the founding laws of a city. In the *Laws*, he imagines an impious youth who adopts the view that the universe emerged into being from the lowest mechanical beginning and only later developed and gave birth to the gods, intelligence and the various arts. To such an arrogant youth, the Athenian Stranger makes the following argument:

> Let us say to the youth: The ruler of the universe has ordered all things with a view to the excellence and preservation of the whole, and each part, as far as may be, has an action and passion appropriate to it. Over these, down to the least fraction of them, ministers have been appointed to preside, who have wrought out their perfection with infinitesimal exactness. And one of these portions of the universe is thine own, unhappy man, which, however little, contributes to the whole; and you do not seem to be aware that this and every other creation is for the sake of the whole, and in order that the life of the whole may be blessed; and that you are created for the sake of the whole, and not the whole for the sake of you. For every physician and every skilled artist does all things for the sake of the whole, directing his effort towards the common good, executing the part for the sake of the whole, and not the whole for the sake of the part. And you are annoyed because you are ignorant how what is best for you happens to you and to the universe, as far as the laws of the common creation admit.[105]

The impiety of this imaginary youth lies in him supposing he is the centre of existence, and that the universe exists for his sake, and not, rather, that he exists for the sake of the good of the whole. For the ancient philosophers, such an introverted view of things is the root of all ignorance. From such a position there cannot be any real enquiry into the nature of things, or into the true nature of society. The great cosmic order is not governed by mere mechanical laws, but, rather, it is directed to an end where every part may fulfil its own nature through contributing to the whole. And what each human being may contribute to the whole resides in their gifts or talents. Thus, "every physician and every skilled artist does all things for the sake of the whole, directing his effort towards the common good." Plato likens the lawmaker to the physician, for laws are a kind of political medicine for remedying the ailments that can befall society. And, like medicine, its remedies are for the sake of the good health of the whole. And this is brought about through the citizens being ever-conscious of the relation of the city to the cosmos from which it derives its pattern.

ALL THINGS INCLINE TO THE GOOD

In the ancient understanding of Nature, or the cosmos, everything is in motion towards its proper end. Thus, Plato says each part, "has an action and passion appropriate to it." Everything seeks the fulfilment of its being through its own natural inclination towards its appropriate end, and this end is its essential nature made manifest in its flowering or completion. The "action and passion appropriate" to the human being manifests in the inclination to seek wisdom and to live justly. And the love of justice is the root of all ethics and insight into politics. The human being by nature desires to live in a just society and in the company of good citizens. There is an innate knowledge that this is the happiest state of life and the most peaceful, and where the inner life and the outer life accord with one another.

Everything in the cosmos unfolds towards its proper end because all things are ruled by intelligence, the cosmos itself being intelligent, contrary to the opinion of Plato's impious youth. This understanding that the cosmos was intelligent and wise passed down from Plato and Aristotle to the Stoics as their essential key to ethics. Cicero records the philosophy of the Stoics in his *On the Nature of the Gods*, where he writes:

> One can also see that the cosmos contains intelligence from the fact that it is without doubt better than any other nature.

> Just as there is no part of our body which is not of less value
> than we ourselves are, so the cosmos as a whole must be of
> more value than any part of it. But if this is so, the cosmos
> must necessarily be wise, for if it were not, then human beings,
> who are part of the cosmos, would have to be of more value
> than the entire cosmos in virtue of participation in reason.[106]

Human beings have reason as a gift of cosmic reason, so that they may
contemplate the order, wisdom, and goodness of the cosmos. Through this
gift, human nature is enabled to act in accord with the cosmic wisdom.
To act thus, as Plato says, is to live in justice. For one of the meanings of
the ancient word *kosmos* is justice, its opposite being *chaos*, injustice. Justice
within the soul is temperance, which arises through the outer virtues of
courage and prudence. Without these virtues, human beings cannot direct
themselves towards what is good, wise, or just. As the Stoics put it:

> The goal of all these virtues is to live consistently with
> nature. Each one enables a human being to achieve this
> [goal] in his own way; for [a human] has from nature
> inclinations to discover what is appropriate and to stabilize
> his impulses and to stand firm and to distribute [fairly]. And
> each of the virtues does what is consonant [with these
> inclinations] and does its own job, thus enabling a human
> being to live consistently with nature.[107]

What is true for an individual is likewise true for a society, it being an
image of the soul writ large. The soul that is just can perceive universal
justice and contemplate it. This perception confers a special gift of discernment in the course of things: "... only the virtuous man is a prophet since
he has a knowledge which distinguishes the signs relevant to human life
which come from the gods and daimons."[108] The virtuous soul, because it
is able to act in accord with the order of the whole, is able to act for the
common good of the society through true understanding. It has the special
gift of foresight, the capacity to discern the future effects of actions and
of law-making. The soul deficient in virtue cannot act for the greater good
due to a lack of this kind of perception. In the Stoic view, a soul without
virtue is an incomplete soul and hardly human.

Since each individual is part of the greater community of the city and of the cosmos, the good or just action of that one person brings benefit to all. This is because goodness and justice are universals that all things participate in. Plutarch says: "If a single sage anywhere at all extends his finger prudently, all sages throughout the inhabited world are benefited."[109] And he also speaks of, "The amazing benefit which sages receive from the virtuous motions of one another even if they are not together and happen not even to be acquainted."

For the ancient philosophers, there can be no such thing as 'private morality' or personal moral values, since all moral actions arise from participation in the cosmic order. From this ancient perspective, the moral relativism of modernity is simply not morality at all. This is because, as we have seen, good or just actions derive from the universal goodness and justice which already govern the whole cosmos. To perform a good act is to share in the universal good, to abide with the universal intelligence or *logos*. The ground of ethics is the well-being of the whole, just as the ground of wisdom is knowledge of the whole. To act virtuously is to act in accord with human nature, most especially with reason which the human soul shares with the cosmos and the gods.

TRUE CITIZENSHIP

The Stoics speak of two types of cities – one is in the universe, the dwelling place of the gods, and the other lies within human cities. Insofar as human beings act wisely and virtuously, they dwell in both cities at once. No one speaks of this more eloquently than Cicero:

> The universe is as it were a city consisting of gods and men, the gods exercising leadership, the men subordinate. Community exists between them because they partake of reason, which is natural law; and all else has come into being for their sake. In consequence of which it must be believed that the god who administers the whole exercises providence for men, being beneficent, kind, well-disposed to men, just and having all the virtues.[110]

It is this universal providence that is the ground of the unity of the human community. Unity springs from the highest principle, "But those who have reason in common also have right reason in common. Since that is law, we men must also be reckoned to be associated with the gods in law. But further, those who have these things in common must be held to belong to the same state (*civitas*)."[111]

Those who have reason in common, and who live justly, are by definition 'citizens'. In such citizenship there is no need for any claims of rights, as happened in the seventeenth century, because universal justice is already given in the nature of things. But this justice may only manifest in human affairs when each seeks the good of all. It then comes into being via peace and friendship, rather than through strife or private claims. There is a remarkable passage in Plato's *Laws* which argues that only when the common good is sought is the political art practiced wisely:

> For, in the first place, it is difficult to know that the true political art must care not for the private but for the common – for the common binds cities together, while the private tears them apart – and that it is in the interest of both the common and the private that the common, rather than the private be established nobly.[112]

In truth, the true and final aim of law is friendship, as Plato says in the *Laws*: "When we asserted one should look toward moderation, or prudence, or friendship, these goals are not different but the same."[113] Friendship is the crown of citizenship. Aristotle says there can be no injustice between true friends, and that only friends are truly citizens.[114]

It is clear, then, that the ancients held that human nature may fulfil itself only through coming into harmony with the whole, the citizen with the city and all humanity, and the city and all humanity with the cosmos and the gods. Only through contemplating the heavens may the human person come to self-knowledge. The 'private self' of secular modernity is really a delusion and ultimately nihilistic. By its nature the soul yearns for what transcends it, and is completed through what transcends it. As Aristotle says at the opening of *Metaphysics*: "All human beings by nature stretch themselves toward knowing."[115]

THE GROUND OF LOVE

This 'stretching toward knowing' is a key to both the philosophical and religious understanding of love. The soul already loves what transcends it, and, in this way, it belongs to truth or wisdom or goodness, even prior to belonging to itself. Aquinas puts this very powerfully in his *Summa Theologica*:

> Now by nature every creature by being himself belongs to God; so that natural love of angels and men is first and foremost for God and then for themselves. If it were not so, their natural love would be perverse and would have to be destroyed rather than fulfilled by the love of charity. One naturally loves oneself more than something else of equal rank because one is more united to oneself, but if the other thing is the entire ground of one's own existence and goodness then by nature one loves it more than oneself: by nature parts love the whole more than themselves, and individuals the good of the species more than their individual good. God however is not only the good of a species but good as such and for all; and so by nature everything loves God in its own way more than itself.

As the philosopher, Pierre Manent, observes, it is the distance between our immediate sense of being and the transcendent that makes us human:

> It is the distance between his empirical, real being, and the end he pursues – justice, wisdom, truth – a distance that is recognised so as to be eliminated, and yet always invincibly maintained by reason of the 'sinful' or simply 'intermediary' character of man, that opens a space where he can reflect on himself and recognize himself as man.[116]

It is this openness to transcendence, to what lies beyond our immediate grasp, that makes us human. The ends that call us – 'justice, wisdom, truth' – also remind us of our finitude because we cannot immediately accomplish these ends, and this also is what makes us human. This finitude is traditionally expressed in many different symbols, such as sin or the Fall, loss or alienation, or of the soul descending into a mortal body, none of which are to be taken literally. Nevertheless, this distance from arriving at justice, wisdom and truth is crossed over by love – because our being already loves these things. Our human finitude is overcome through love of the infinite. And so Aquinas says that, in the depths of every creature's being, each loves God before itself, because love loves what is ultimate and whole first. From that love each creature then loves itself in the right manner *as belonging to God*. In this way, each creature loves and acts for the good of the whole and so is given to itself through the whole. Love recognises that being or existence is a gift, and cannot be grasped properly otherwise.

Insofar as the Enlightenment conferred upon human nature self-sovereignty and the social contract, it abandoned the soul's openness to transcendence and the cosmic law that draws all beings towards their true fulfilment in true community. Under the spell of this delusory notion of human nature, the industrial consumer society arose, grounded in mutual competition, rather than in the common good, and so necessarily now the human lives in endless discontent, hoping to overcome the distance between empirical being and fulfilment through endless appropriation of artificial products.

The difficulty, from the modern perspective, is that the human will is no longer understood to be rooted in love. Instead, it is taken to be self-seeking, and instead of conforming itself to the natural order of things, it attempts to gain mastery over them. This is more than simply a moral question, although it is that too. It is ultimately a mystical question. Meister Eckhart says:

> Now you may ask when the will is a right will. The will is perfect and right when it is without all attachment, when it has gone out of self and is shaped and formed after the will of God. The more this is so, the more perfect and true the will. And with *that* will you can do anything, love or anything else.[117]

Just as knowledge attains its end only through being ruled by the truth of things, so the will attains its end only through being ruled by the divine will. That will is freedom. Once the soul assents to the infinite goodness of the divine will, it is then enabled to witness goodness everywhere:

But God's will has savour for me only in that unity wherein the repose of God's goodness is in all creatures, in which it reposes with everything that ever had being and life, as in its final end: *there* you should love the Holy Ghost, as he is in union – not on his own, but where he has the taste of God's goodness alone in unity, whence all goodness flows from the superfluity of God's goodness.[118]

To 'savour' God's goodness abiding in all creatures involves granting to all creatures their true end in God. This 'granting' is a true act of will, grounded in love. According to Eckhart, the mystical apprehension of the divine in the created cosmos is possible only when things are known and loved for their own sake. And loving them for their own sake is possible only through loving God before all else. Then, according to Eckhart, it is possible to see how the great laws of the universe draw every creature towards its proper end:

You must know that all creatures strive and work naturally to become like God. The heavens would not revolve if they did not pursue or seek for God, or a likeness to God. If God were not in all things, nature would cease operation and not strive for anything; for, whether you like it or not, and whether you know it or not, nature secretly and in her inmost parts seeks and aims at God.[119]

In Eckhart's view, just as with Plato, Aristotle, and the Stoics, everything in nature aims at the good, or perfection, or likeness to God. These terms are saying the same thing in the distinct language or symbols of each tradition. The key is to understand nature as oriented towards fulfilment. This teleological view of nature, which endured through the Middle Ages, was denied by the philosophers of the seventeenth and eighteenth centuries, and so a *lower aim* had to be given to the world and to every living being, including the human race. In social thought, this begins with Machiavelli, who discounted the ancient philosophers and medieval scholastics as impractical utopian dreamers. The 'real world' must be negotiated through compromise. But this new lower aim, which sought to be practical, makes a promise it cannot fulfil, because human nature and society cannot find rest or fulfilment through aiming at less than the true ends every being aspires towards. So the pursuit of material wealth replaced the pursuit of the common good, and the pursuit of private happiness replaced community and the noble life of friendship. Citizenship, in the ancient sense, was abandoned. Yet everyone knows in their hearts that this great compromise is wrong and out of joint with Nature, and so our age lives in a perpetual conflict between its received materialist ideology and the inner knowledge of the soul. This conflict is the spiritual crisis of our age.

TRUE PEACEFULNESS

Human nature cannot find peace through aiming at less than its true calling. It will necessarily remain restless otherwise. This is the insight that unites the ancient philosophers, as well as the great religions. To quote Meister Eckhart once again:

> St. Dionysius says divine peace pervades and orders and ends all things; if peace did not do this, all things would be dissipated and there would be no order. Secondly, peace causes creatures to pour themselves out and flow in love and without harm. Thirdly, it makes creatures serviceable to one another, so that they have a support in one another. What one of them cannot have of itself, it gets from another. Thus one creature derives from another. Fourthly, it makes them turn back to their original source, which is God.[120]

In those few words, Eckhart says it all.

What emerges from all we have said is that everything depends on what we are dedicated to. The philosopher asks what should be sought above all else, and it is the truth of things. In seeking the truth, the question becomes refined into, "How to live in accord with truth?" Morally, this means living justly because action in justice is action in accord with the true order of things – what we called at the outset the cosmic harmony. This gentle enquiry into truth is the proper work of all humanity, not just of the great philosophers. Where this work is done, civilisation flowers, as we see in the time of Plato in Greece, or Confucius in China, or the Lord Buddha in India. The enquiry into truth cannot be separated from the enquiry into goodness. The intellect rests in truth and the heart or will in goodness, and justice unites them. This is why justice is at once a virtue, a knowledge and an activity. It is an inexhaustible enquiry.

Yet the philosophers aspire beyond all practical matters to pure contemplation, to unite the mind with truth and rest there, unmoved by any further desire. It is here where the philosopher and the mystic draw together. For the mystic sees the ineffable present everywhere, and that the divine goodness is what enlivens and draws all things into order and towards their fulfilment. It is truth and goodness that act everywhere – what the ancients called divine providence. The eternal and the temporal are mysteriously made one. Seeing all this, and abiding in the presence of God, the mystic is at peace inwardly and outwardly, and has no desire to do anything without God's bidding.

The life of the philosopher and the mystic are shining examples of how we ought to live. The key is what the heart is set on. What the heart dedicates itself to will determine its way of life and what it may bring to the world. This is the work we are called to by nature. It is an ongoing work, just as a mother's care for her child is an ongoing work. Unlike the materialist ideology, it does not claim to solve all problems and bring satisfaction through a final conquest of Nature. It is that ideology that is a false utopia. The true work is an ongoing work both within and without, of bringing order in the soul in its different parts, and order in action through justice towards all things. Without undertaking this work, humankind cannot live in peace, but when seeking the true and the good, peace comes unbidden as a gift of grace.

99. Plato, Translated by Benjamin Jowett, 1920, *Timaeus*, New York: Random House, 47.

100. Cicero, *De Finibus*, III, 20-21.

101. See Eric Voegelin, 1987, *The New Science of Politics: An Introduction*, University of Chicago Press, 61 for a full discussion of this in Plato's conception of the polis.

102. Maulana Karenga, 2004, *Maat, The Moral Ideal in Ancient Egypt: A Study in Classical*

African Ethics. London: Routledge, 257.

103. Ibid, 258.

104. Ibid, 381.

105. Plato, Translated by B Jowett, *Laws*, 903b.

106. *The Stoic Reader*, Translated by B Inwood and L Gerson, 2008, Hackett Publishing Company, 65.

107. Ibid, 126.

108. Ibid, 150.

109. Ibid, 100.

110. Malcolm Schofield, 1999, *The Stoic Idea of the City*, Chicago: University of Chicago Press, 66.

111. Ibid, 68.

112. Plato, Translated by Thomas Pangle, 1980, *The Laws of Plato*, New York: Basic Books, 875a.

113. Ibid, 693c.

114. See Aristotle, Translated by Joe Sachs, 2002, *Nicomachean Ethics*, Newburyport, MA: Focus Publishing.

115. Aristotle, Translated by Joe Sachs, 2002, *Metaphysics*, New Mexico: Green Lion Press, Book I.

116. Pierre Manent, 1998, *The City of Man,* New Jersey: Princeton University Press, 136.

117. Meister Eckhart, Trans. by M O'C Walshe, with a Foreword by Bernard McGinn, 2009, *The Complete Mystical Works of Meister Eckhart*, 'The Talks of Instruction', New York: The Crossroad Publishing Company, 595.

118. Ibid, 'Sermon Fifty One', 270.

119. Ibid, 'Sermon Forty Two', 235.

120. Ibid, 'Sermon 26', 168.

CHAPTER **SIX**

PEACEMAKING AND THE FEMININE PRINCIPLE

MARIANNE MARSTRAND

WOMEN CAN PLAY A SIGNIFICANT part in the global peacebuilding process. In fact, women, when enabled and empowered, can be true peacemakers and there are many examples from around the world that demonstrate the importance of applying the feminine principle to peacemaking, which itself is nourished by all faith traditions.

Peacefulness has always been rooted in spiritual traditions – indeed, there are spiritual communities that emphasise the importance of attaining 'inner peace' through the regular practice of reflection, prayer and meditation. Being able to focus the mind and thought is important if we are to effect any outer change in the world. Our actions need to come from a place of deeper wisdom, and learning to sit in silence is essential to access this quiet knowing. If we are able to tap these deeper parts of ourselves, our actions will be clear and purposeful. We will better understand the underlying causes of a dilemma, tension or conflict, as well as knowing how to properly respond.

Most spiritual traditions teach us to meditate and go inwards and emphasise the importance of generating love and compassion. This is where the possibility for meaningful impact grows. With awareness, we see that small actions done with a pure and open heart can unfold with almost miraculous results – whether those results are immediate or take years to come to pass matters not. Having a personal practise that disciplines our erratic thoughts and negative habits helps us see that each act has meaning and makes deep impressions, not only on our own being, but on that of others and the world around us. This suggests that being peace is making peace, the heart of which encompasses the feminine principle.

In this chapter, I draw on my experience working at the Global Peace Initiative of Women (GPIW) and the many stories of women peacemakers I have encountered to illustrate the connection between peacemaking and the feminine principle.

THE GPIW

The Global Peace Initiative of Women (GPIW) was founded in 2002, and is unique in that the vision of this organisation is held and led by women. Initiated by Dena Merriam and a group of senior women faith leaders representing the major world religions, it was created as a response to the lack of real opportunity for women from religious communities to find an international platform to speak about peace. Over the years, we have been honoured to work with many remarkable women, yet whilst the GPIW is guided by women, it is not exclusive. Practical support, monies, spiritual wisdom and direction have been offered by equally remarkable men who we have had the privilege to encounter.

As the war in Iraq escalated and we heard with heavy hearts about the plight of thousands of widows and orphans, it became clear that voices capable of speaking truth to power were needed everywhere, and the voices of women were needed, in particular. One such outspoken voice, who also serves as a Co-Chair of GPIW, is the compassionate and fiery Catholic leader and Benedictine nun, Sister Joan Chittister, who reminds us that if we are to have peace, we need to include women in the decisions that greatly affect our world. Without women, who make up half of humanity, it would be like confronting our daily challenges with only half a body or half a brain. While political leaders address the outer causes of conflicts, women suffer the greatest consequences of war, and so women readily bring back the discussion to concern for the safety of families and children. At our first gathering at the Palais des Nations in Geneva in 2002, Sister Joan Chittister ended her statement in the General Assembly with the words, "It is not about life after death, but about life before death." These words have stayed with me all these years.

Our work primarily began with engaging faith leaders from the world's many traditions, and I became interested in seeing how their practices could flow into our daily lives. As we began to work with women from places of great suffering, this became even more important for me to understand. How do our wisdom traditions help us reawaken our reverence for all of life? How do women, in particular, differ in their ways of bringing peacefulness to their families and communities? Can women help bring about a more embracing worldview, one that is inclusive of the Earth and supportive of all her living systems, our animal relatives, the plants, the trees and waters?

THE FEMININE PRINCIPLE

> And sadly, because our culture has devalued the feminine,
> we have repressed so much of her nature, so many of her
> qualities. Instead we live primarily masculine values; we are
> goal oriented, competitive, driven. Masculine values even
> dominate our spiritual quest; we seek to be better, to
> improve our self, to get somewhere. We have forgotten the
> feminine qualities of waiting, listening, being empty. We
> have dismissed the deep need of the soul, our longing, the
> feminine side of love.
> Llewellyn Vaughan-Lee, *Love is a Fire:*
> *A Sufi's Mystical Path Home*

What is the feminine and what are the qualities of the feminine? Often, the expression 'the feminine' is confused with 'feminism' or 'gender equality', but these are only superficial descriptions of the term. Men and women both hold qualities of the feminine. The feminine knows the value of quiet listening, and that sometimes we must wait patiently. The feminine is inclusive and dislikes hierarchy. Too much grandstanding, egocentric behaviour, or self-serving agendas are not well tolerated. She will respond with absolute justice, humorously at times, if fitting to the situation. She reminds us that it is about the whole and not just the few.

The sacred feminine is about creating connections between people, groups and causes. Llewellyn Vaughan-Lee reminds us that:

> The feminine is more instinctively and naturally attuned to life, its patterns and powers. And feminine consciousness is less dominated by reason, more open to the mystery of the symbolic inner world. The feminine is vital in this work of awakening.[121]

Angela Fischer, a mystic who writes on the sacred feminine and meditation, tells us that it is the feminine that can reconnect us to the soul, our own soul and the soul of the world. This deeper connection is needed if our outer work is to have the real force needed to change society.

Men and women both embody the sacred feminine and it is through these qualities that men and women together can help to create new policy frameworks that contribute to the wellbeing of people, implement new economic systems driven less by personal gain and more by social good, and reorient businesses to do more than make a profit. The feminine is needed to help us redefine development and find the models that sustain and nurture life. The feminine also understands interconnections and relationships and can help us navigate globalisation in beneficial ways by building partnerships and working more collaboratively.

Here are two brief stories to illustrate the working of the feminine in developing kind-heartedness and shaping our peaceful characters.

Amel, a young woman from southern Sudan, described a scene she recalled of donors distributing food aid to villages: "Big trucks drove through, often never stopping, but simply dumping bags of grain on the street for people to come and take as fast as they could." She remembered feeling how little care or respect there was in this exchange. It not only belittled those desperate for the aid, but it deprived the donors of the opportunity to embody their own dignity and experience their charity in a different way. The feminine really embodies care and caring and by embracing feminine principles, our well-meaning activities can be further enriched and will touch the hearts of those whom we serve.

A young couple moved to Bologna and did not know anyone on their new street. They created a Facebook page for the street and put up posters to let the residents know their interest in connecting. It was not long before people were connecting, faces became familiar and the new residents enjoyed friendly greetings and new encounters with their neighbours. Much more followed. They began helping one another with simple tasks, shopping for an older person alone at home, delivering a meal or taking someone to the doctor. It was a simple idea and it had remarkable consequences. Human interaction, companionship and friendship are treasures and the feminine can help show us the inherent value of the universal truth of interconnection.

BEAUTY, HARMONY AND PEACE IN OUR SURROUNDINGS

The feminine is needed at this time to help us create beauty and the harmony needed to feel at peace. We are losing the ability to appreciate beauty. Not the beauty of fashion magazines or expensive cars, but the inherent beauty that is found in all of Nature in the movement and softness of light, natural surroundings, harmonious sound and colours, and crystal clear waters.

In Western culture in particular, there is a great loss in this respect. In most urban areas, we are surrounded by buildings and structures built mainly for function or based on cost concerns with little thought as to how they affect the harmony of a place, our mood, or how they organise us. Do they bring us together around fountains or in plazas at the end of the day to laugh and talk, or do they isolate and separate us in their functionality? We have allowed ourselves to be surrounded by sounds, noises, even music, that is irritating to the spirit, and, to cope, we eventually must either tune them out or become desensitised.

How does it affect us – all these advertisements, factories, trucks, sirens, loudspeakers and humming air conditioners? And what of the invisible frequencies of electromagnetic radiation, Wi-Fi, signals from satellites and cell phone towers that pass unseen through the air, the walls and our bodies? All of this affects us. It disorients birds and bees, and perhaps is one cause of their drastic declines in populations.

The Earth holds a healing frequency that the human body responds to and harmoniously resonates with, but this is more and more difficult in the midst of the many overpowering negative frequencies. This is skilfully explained in the film *Resonance: Beings of Frequency* by James Russel. Awareness of our exposure and overreliance on technology allows us to take necessary precautions. When we convene circles or meetings, we look for places in natural surroundings. Spirit needs space to move freely to connect the hearts of those in the circle and to create relationships and bonds among those gathered. Create beauty. This brings peacefulness.

A certain lack of attention to our habits has caused us to lose much of what connects us to the deeper dimensions of life. Perhaps our greatest loss is the loss of our connection to Nature. When we come out of balance with the natural forces of the universe that govern life, we weaken not only our bodies, but our hearts and minds – making us vulnerable to forces that hinder us from living up to our highest human potential and from being the majestic creatures we are. We have allowed much to stifle the human spirit, opened ourselves to being mesmerised by what some call 'mind control devices' – our televisions, tablets, and smartphones. Time that we can never regain is often frittered away interacting with screens. It is easy to get caught up in the endless stream of entertainment available now. This constant artificial interaction affects not only our awareness, attention span, and memory, but the cognitive ability of our complex and fragile minds – minds we need to safeguard and protect in order to live peacefully. We thoughtlessly give these devices to young children as toys, not fully understanding the far-reaching consequences this may have.

In Thailand, a Buddhist teacher and nun has created a *Dharma* centre and haven of natural beauty. Mae Chee Sansanee was at one time a famous and successful Thai actress. Circumstances created a completely new direction for her and she decided to take monastic vows and became a Buddhist nun. She gave up a glamorous lifestyle and devoted her attention to helping others. She teaches through example as she rallies students and volunteers to join in her social activism and peace-building work. She has taken on pressing social issues, including the Buddhist-Muslim tensions in Southern Thailand. Her centre, an oasis on the outskirts of Bangkok, has become a place to heal a broken human, whether from poverty, the trauma of prostitution, or the damaged young souls who are victims of human trafficking for sex or slave labour.

At Sathira-Dhammasathan, she shelters, educates and feeds with her loving-kindness those who come. On several acres, she has created a temple compound of exquisite beauty that leaves you breathless. Wooden Thai style buildings and other creative infrastructure has been crafted by hand, mostly by volunteers, under the love and care of Mae Chee's great artistry and sensitivity. To walk inside her Tara temple is to enter the world of the Goddess. As one strolls the walkways and paths, one encounters lotus ponds, Thai structures in carved wood, flower gardens and lawns, great trees around which kindergarten children gather in the morning. The Buddha statue is perched into the winding branches of the great Bodhi tree as if it is miraculously and naturally emerging from its trunk. It is a sanctuary of healing for the body and soul, and those who come experience this. Such an environment allows for seeds to grow, whether in the soil, or in the human heart. Fresh and natural food is cooked and served and one feels rejuvenated by the abundance of Nature. We look for complex solutions to our present-day problems, but often the solution is close at hand and simple, we have just forgotten. By surrounding ourselves with what is more natural to life, our human spirit resonates with this instinctively and an alignment with what is already in harmony can occur.

GATHER, ENCOUNTER AND LISTEN

Other feminine modes of peacebuilding we see more and more of are the many interfaith groups that are widening their boundaries and befriending other traditions. In this discovery of one another they find shared purpose and experiences — a certain relief in giving up rigid dogmas that close the mind. It is powerful to take part in these gatherings as different faiths sit together in silence, or join for discussion on pressing issues. When women and men gather, and listen to each other, they can help to break down barriers by having the courage to reach out to the 'other'. It is encouraging to see interfaith and inter-spiritual groups growing and spreading.

The feminine also makes it possible for human beings to develop powerful peacemaking initiatives born out of personal loss and tragedy. When individuals, through their own loss or grief, are stripped down, bared to the soul in their pain, when everything one cares about is taken away, when a person is left with only enough strength for the things in life that really count, the feminine can stimulate a profound reverence, so that life can emerge from the ruins. It is often in such encounters, in listening to pain, loss and suffering that we can truly resume our faith in humanity.

In this way, as we have seen again and again, lifelong friendships between so-called enemies have come about as a result of meeting and listening in person. For instance, the Parents Circle Family Forum in Israel/Palestine brings together bereaved relatives who have lost loved ones to violence in the Middle East, and, in Rwanda, after the genocide in 1994, the Rwandan Widows' Association was formed by women who came together, Hutus and Tutsis, sharing and listening to each other's grief and collectively raising the orphans of this genocide. When such stories are shared, tens of thousands can benefit from listening to the pain and loving courage of a single individual.

Listening to a younger generation is now increasingly a priority where our modern world of fragmentation can easily make these individuals feel alienated, and where education is more geared to passing exams than engaging with young people, or sharing great human stories. A young journalist was worried about his friend who had become radical and joined with separatists. "Why?" the journalist asked his friend. His friend shared a typical story: before radicalisation, he felt he was a 'nobody', insignificant and without a voice. Now that he was part of something larger, he felt that he had received recognition and that people had to pay attention to him, even if it was often out of fear. The young journalist was stunned. Where were the mentors around this young man who could tell their stories of life? Where were the evenings around a fire when the village elders and wise men and women shared their life experiences that touched on human values and perennial truths? This young man's process of being radicalised also begs a question about how we might create the conditions for human encounters and listening, so that there is more engagement and more meaningful involvement for young people, rather than alienation and disillusionment.

CREATE AND ENLARGE RELATIONAL CIRCLES

The feminine can help create a circle and bring people closer into relationships. This is done by engendering a space of respect and authenticity.

In 2009, the GPIW held a dialogue in Kashmir and brought together young people from three different regions. The state is divided physically by terrain and mountain passes, as well as religiously, so that, in the Kashmir valley, you can find Muslims, whilst the Ladakh region is predominantly Buddhist and south of Srinagar, in Jammu, there is a Hindu community. More than 200 young people joined us for the two-day programme and they were offered the podium to speak.

A young exuberant woman from Jammu said it was her first time speaking to other Kashmiris in an open manner and she spoke of her love for Kashmir and how she longed for more interaction amongst the people of the various regions that feel so divided. Her voice broke and she cried because she had, for so long, wished for a chance to voice this longing for the unity she imagines for Kashmir. Bringing people into the circle is the work of the feminine.

In 2004, we travelled to the Middle East. Ambitious, hopeful and naïve, we brought together 270 women from Israel and Palestine to meet for three days near the Dead Sea in Jordan. Invitations had gone out and seven or more women members of the Israeli Knesset agreed to come. Women rabbis and writers, artists and peacemakers came. Women leaders from Palestinian civil society, as well as community organisers, members of religious communities, Muslim and Christians from Ramallah and Gaza, also agreed to join. Many of the women had been working towards peace for years, opening channels of communication.

Just prior to the gathering, the borders around the Gaza Strip had been shut down almost completely due to a recent attack. This presented a problem for the 14 women who were ready to join us. They had not been out of the Gaza Strip for several years, some of them being thus separated from close friends and relatives. The situation seemed impossible to resolve and we did not know how to help them until one of the Israeli coordinators said her uncle happened to work at one of the checkpoints and she would call him. She called and asked that he let the women through and he did – a small miracle during a time of great mistrust and fear.

At the gathering, we were all together talking and listening to stories. There were tears and moments of anger and accusation, but there was equally much smiling and laughter. Above all, we learned of the inventive and no-nonsense ways that women, on both sides, worked towards peace from the ground up. I watched the skillful way in which our Chair, Rev.

Joan Brown Campbell, with her genuine warmth and grandmotherly manner, could calm down the room if things got out of hand and when too many were speaking or even shouting at once. I would see her work this magic again years later when we brought Iraqi women to New York City at the height of the war there.

Toward the end of our days near the Dead Sea, many friendships were formed, which are lasting to this day. The programme ended with the joining of hands in the plenary hall and singing 'We Shall Overcome'. From the sidelines, the Israeli doctor who regularly travelled with the Knesset members asked me how this was done. In 15 years of travelling to such peace meetings, he had not experienced anything like this. He was emotional and much moved.

The feminine understands that we cannot force others to make peace, but we can guide them into a circle where peace is felt, where there is an opening for it to grow and surround us in its essential truth. Who doesn't want peace? Who doesn't want to feel loved? Warmth and kindness and noble intentions help create spaces that allow ideas and personal connections to emerge with their own power – then we can be in for unexpected surprises. We have found that opening a circle with sacred music from the region, prayers offered from different traditions, stories or a reading that touches the heart can bring people into their own hearts far quicker than a speech read from a podium. If we are trying to move people's hearts, then let's use skillful means to do just that. We cannot control everything, but we can create a space that reflects human dignity and values, one that is blessed with loving persons, wise persons, generous persons, inspiring persons; those people we know and meet who hold a love for humanity and yet wish for nothing in return. Invite such persons into the circle, whether they hold big titles or not. They need to be present and their presence will have an effect.

TRUST IN A 'HUMAN KEY'

Women came to the rescue when a meeting we had been working on for many months collapsed in a logistical nightmare just a few short weeks before the major event. It required us to surrender in trust and willingness to allow for something new and different to take the place of what had been so carefully planned. I have seen this happen on many occasions in different ways – it is as if some unseen hand steps in and brushes away all you have done and then says, "No, no, no … let's do it like this and it will be even better." While a masculine approach would have been to hold firm and push for the old plan, the feminine is better able to remain open to the unexpected. Flexibility can be very helpful. We may take the risk of looking a bit more disorganised, but, in fact, the organisation can become more finely in tune with what would be of real benefit for all, however that transpires. This requires the feminine quality of waiting and listening.

This striking example happened in 2010 when we organised for a delegation of senior religious leaders to travel to South Korea to be present during the time of the G20 Summit in Seoul. We were not part of the official meetings with the heads of state who had come together to discuss the global financial situation, but part of a parallel event. We were there to discuss alternative economic models. We had the funding and our planning was ahead of schedule. A site visit was made to Seoul months before the event to research hotels and meeting venues and look for like-minded organisations to partner with us. We had confirmed a block of rooms for our delegation at the Hilton hotel and had even been offered the meeting hall of one of the largest Buddhist orders of monks in South Korea. All was set and our sponsor organisation in Japan was pleased with the prestigious arrangements.

Three weeks before the event though, everything fell apart. Our hotel rooms were cancelled as they were requisitioned by the US delegation and, when a day or so later, the monks said the meeting room was no longer available, we were horror-stricken. With one fell swoop, everything was dismantled – all that we had carefully planned and constructed over many months unravelled before our eyes. However, we had seen this happen before and had learned to allow the space and flexibility for such disruption – for what we had also noticed is that the outcome of the new design is more than often far better than we could have ever organised ourselves.

There is always a 'human key' – a kind-spirited individual who can open a doorway to a nexus of fellow supporters. It is important to recognise such individuals for they are usually not the ones to bring attention to themselves. We met Mrs Kim on our first site visit through a friend. We did not know her well, but liked her practical way. She was funny too. She trusted us and we trusted her. She could move with ease in many circles. In desperation, we called her from the US and said that we needed help to reorganise the whole programme. The only thing confirmed were the 20 or so religious leaders who were holding air tickets and eagerly looking forward to being in Seoul during the Summit. Mrs Kim asked that we fly back to South Korea immediately and that she would host some women for a breakfast meeting and see what could be done.

The flight landed and breakfast was held a few hours after at the home of Mrs Kim. One could see she was much admired by the women who joined us. Each woman introduced herself, sometimes through another woman interpreting in English. One was a professor at the Buddhist University and offered their shrine hall for a day, saying the university would be honoured and would even send participants. Another said she was a professional interpreter and volunteered to translate for the religious leaders. Another arranged flowers for major events, and yet another had a friend who had a major television talk show and wanted our founder to come and tell several million viewers about the role of faith leaders in the G20 and what we meant by alternative economics. It was like the Knights of the Round Table, each bearing a gift or talent or connection that would culminate in several days of events far beyond any of our expectations. A quiet woman spoke last and said her teacher, a Buddhist nun, would also like to help.

Daehaeng Kun Sunim, who has since passed on, was a much loved Buddhist nun and Zen master. At an advanced age and in poor health, she now lived in seclusion at her monastery outside Seoul. Without ever meeting us, Daehaeng Kun Sunim told the senior abbess, "These women are working for the same purpose we are and therefore we must help them."

A rain of blessings fell everywhere and suddenly we had hundreds of volunteers preparing the meeting halls, as well as radio and newspaper interviews, banquet lunches, and visits to thousand-year old monasteries where more banquets awaited our group. On the final day, Daeheng Kun Sunim supplied us with four buses to take our delegation to the DMZ, the demilitarised buffer zone that divides North and South Korea, together with 200 South Koreans, who had never been allowed there. Off limits to most, Mrs Kim had secured permission with the general in charge and 200 names were submitted for clearance. A session was held in the glass hall that overlooks North Korea. Each leader offered their prayers for peace and, as a final parting gift, Daehaeng Kun Sunim sent a troupe of Korean dancers, national treasures recognised by UNESCO, to offer the grand finale, an exquisite dance for peace, most probably also enjoyed by a curious North Korean military through their telescopes. The power of their dance and the sound of the drums in tune to the precise choreographed steps was full of an energy that moved the hearts of those in the room beyond what speeches and words had already done. Their ritual called in unseen angels to bless the day, to bless the idea of peace between the North and South.

The gifts of Mrs Kim and Daehaeng Kun Sunim and the 100 or more women (and men!) who magically stepped forward to help us in South Korea were actions rooted in the feminine. Their networks and relationships were made available to us — voluntarily, in the spirit of service. They did not know us and they did not know that much about our organisation. We were hampered by a language barrier and this meant so much had to happen through the heart's knowing, through an intuitive trust and feeling.

THE EARTH

Over the last few years, our work has turned more to the Earth. As rivers called out to us, She called us. It feels the most vital contribution we can make during this time when we are at a crossroads and so much is out of balance. Women have come to us to share dreams and vivid real life experiences of hearing the cries of the Earth. One such experience was shared with our group in Greece in 2013, where we came together at the height of the Greek financial crisis.

At breakfast after our first night spent at the quiet mountain hotel on the hillsides of Delphi, Angela Fischer, a mystic and author of writings on the feminine, came to our table. She looked distressed and relayed that the Earth had a message for us. We listened as she recounted her vivid experience of the night. "I was wandering on this beautiful land, the landscape of mountains and valleys, when I suddenly felt a deep pain – an impersonal pain that spread throughout my body. I became aware of a woman lying in a small hollow carved into the land. She was very pale and fragile, it was as if she was dying and suffering deeply. In my heart I knew she was the 'Mother of All', the Earth herself. In the vision experience, I saw people walking over her, not noticing that they were stepping on her. They seemed to be only half-awake, talking all the time, unaware of where they were walking. I saw all the shoes, the boots, continually stepping over her. I was drawn to get closer to her. For a moment, I was alone with her, and I tried to speak to her. But she did not answer. She was frail and in much pain. So I sat down and listened and felt for her.

"After a while she began to speak. She said, 'Don't play around. FEEL. You need to FEEL. Wake up and feel.' I asked her about her pain. She answered, and the deeper we went in conversation, the more she seemed to come alive, the stronger her voice grew. 'My deepest pain is that I no longer can nourish you. My breasts are running dry, my fountains drying out.'

"'What can we do?' I asked. 'Sit with me in the places of darkness,' she replied. And what she didn't say in words, but what I understood through feeling was the need for us to sit there with the light that is within, at the places we do not want to see. I still felt tremendous pain, almost unbearable pain. I felt it in the whole of my being and in my physical body. There seemed to be no escaping it, as if it was imprisoning me and all doors were closed. I cannot recall ever having ever felt this kind of pain, this deep suffering." Angela finished describing her experience. "Still sitting beside her, after some time, I heard the following words in my heart, 'There is love, nothing but love, at the core of creation.' And this was the only door."

We have shared Angela's experience in other gatherings. It brings up resistance. It is difficult to hear how much the Earth is in distress. We want to stay only in the light and not acknowledge there are the dark places that call us to be living witnesses – places of desecration, places of sorrow and grief, so much abuse in both the outer places and inner places. The same impulse that causes violence against women is the same impulse that is causing ecological destruction. There is peace to be made with the Earth. The Earth gives life to everything. She is the nurturer. When we harm the Earth or harm women, we suppress life-giving forces and energy. Our awareness of this spiritual imbalance – the disturbance of our collective mindset – is growing, as is our awareness of the need for healing. Becoming more aware of the sacredness of all of life is imperative; understanding that even our smallest actions and attitudes affect the whole is vital. The feminine can remind us of the care we long for and that we too can offer this to others.

PEACEFULNESS AND THE FEMININE

In Angela's experience the Earth spoke clearly about what this journey of healing requires — we are 'to feel'. We are being asked to come back to being fully human and all the self-respect this entails. When we can own our human dignity again, it will change how we treat one another, how we treat children, how we treat the animals, the forests and rivers. We will come to realise how each of our small actions count. Women show us again and again that when there is an urgency, we can pool our resources, join our talents and put aside any need for credit or glory. The simple joy of being human, of truly being alive will be reward enough. The feminine in each of us can guide us to this place of deeper wisdom that understands reverence for life.

---

121. Llewellyn Vaughan-Lee, 2007, *The Alchemy of Light*, Golden Sufi Center Publishers.

PART III

PART III

MAKING PEACE GLOBALLY

INTRODUCTION

IN THE FIRST TWO PARTS of this book, we have explored the inextricable connectedness between our innate peacefulness and harmony found within our communities. In this third and final part, we discuss how we might make peace in the world at large and how the global socio-economic and political systems and institutional practices could create conditions for peace to flourish. Within each of these public domains, we are concerned with values, structures and processes that are required to nurture peacefulness. In rich and diverse voices, our contributors challenge the notion of justice and war, and imagine what peace might look like through the lenses of systems thinking, proposing the principles and values underpinning an economy of peace and exploring how education for peace might further help bring about the global transformation.

In Chapter Seven, Garrett Thomson, CEO of the Guerrand Hermès Foundation for Peace and Compton Professor of Philosophy at the College of Wooster, Ohio, draws our attention to the nature of conflict in peaceful relations. By arguing that all relations between individuals, groups, institutions and social systems necessarily involve conflict, he suggests that making peace should focus on strengthening and developing richer and more enabling relationships through dialogue, encounter, healing past traumas and more.

In Chapter Eight, Steve Killelea, the Founder and Executive Chairman of Institute for Economics and Peace, argues that systems thinking can give rise to a positive peace framework which outlines the attitudes, institutions and structures – the key interdependent pillars that are necessary to sustain peaceful societies. He suggests that by monitoring and fostering these societal pillars for peace, we can support a virtuous and self-reinforcing cycle of transformation.

In Chapter Nine, Stewart Wallis, economist and former Director of the New Economics Foundation, critiques the neoliberal conception of the market economy and how it encourages greed, selfishness, competitiveness, and injustice – the perfect breeding ground for violence. He then proposes the values and principles upon which a peaceful economy would be built and suggests possible institutional frameworks for such a system.

In Chapter Ten, Mark Milton and Vicki McCoy of Education 4 Peace, report on educational practices aimed at raising awareness amongst young people concerning the importance of emotional wellbeing as the basis for cultivating our inner sense of peacefulness. This is a key to *being peace* and the basis of making peace.

Once again, in this part of the book, our focus continues to be on how the unfolding of our internal qualities of peacefulness contributes to manifestations of peace in the interdisciplinary realms of our relational practices. In this way, the chapters in this final part provide convincing arguments and illustrations that show how, by applying the core values of love, respect, compassion, and justice in our socio-economic and political systems and by strengthening humanising structures and processes globally, we can create the necessary conditions to support a heightened sense of spiritual peace.

CHAPTER **SEVEN**

TOWARDS A THEORY OF PEACEFUL RELATIONS

GARRETT THOMSON

EVEN IF PEACE IS PRIMARILY a spiritual or psychological state, nevertheless, we also need to conceive of peacefulness as a set of social relations, including those that a person has with him/herself. In other words, if peacefulness is an inner state, then it will necessarily express itself relationally. A theory of peaceful relations will apply not only to relations between individuals and groups of persons, but it will also be concerned with institutions and with the structures of a society.

This theory will include the core idea that peacefulness is a feature of conflict. All relations between individuals, groups, institutions, and social systems are conflictual. People have different interests and understandings; ineluctably, this means conflict. Thus, peace cannot be defined as a lack of conflict. More than this, relational peacefulness only becomes operative when there is conflict. That is to say, we cannot be in a peaceful relation until we are in conflictual relations.

In part, peacefulness is the quality that allows conflictive relations to exist without displacing the other non-instrumental goods that constitute human flourishing. Such peacefulness implies that conflictive relations won't make destructive waves. For instance, this is embodied in the family when a specific conflict doesn't affect negatively the other good features of family life. Or, for example, when I squabble with a friend, it doesn't affect the friendship. In part, the nature of peacefulness, as a quality of relations, is that it mutes conflicts that would otherwise undermine wellbeing or flourishing.

The aim of this paper is to illustrate how a conception of peacefulness as a spiritual stance has implications for international politics, or more generally for what socio-political-economic structural systems we should live in. Spiritually and morally orientated understandings of peacefulness have political implications, and are not neutral concerning the structural features of society. We need morally attuned understandings of what it means to be peaceful that have socio-political and structural translations. Furthermore, spiritual peacefulness needs a structural expression: peace cannot fully be an actualised condition of the soul unless it is also a condition of the society in which we live.

TRANSCENDING THE EPISTEMOLOGICAL ASYMMETRY

What does it mean to live in peaceful relations? To answer this, we begin with a hugely important contrast. On the one side, we humans are subject to a systematic epistemological asymmetry. This is the tendency, in our own case, to only see our own good intentions, but in the case of others, to perceive only the results of their actions (which are often bad). This means that we are prone to apply a double standard: we judge ourselves by our good intentions, and others by the results of their actions. This means that I am disposed to see my own actions as always good at heart, and those of others as wrong or, at best, as far from perfect.

On the other side, whenever someone wants something, necessarily they want it under some description that renders it desirable. This doesn't mean that the thing wanted really is desirable, but it does imply that it is perceived as such by the person who wants it. This has profound implications for understanding others: it means that, to comprehend another, we must see the person's intentions under the descriptions that make sense to them from their point of view. There is a way of seeing what the other person wants as good. To desire something is *ipso facto* to see it as desirable.

The juxtaposition of these two points reveals why we humans are systematically susceptible to misunderstanding others. The first indicates that we are disposed to ignore precisely what the second outlines as a condition for understanding others. Having peaceful relations with others requires overcoming this tension. Let us illustrate this. I quarrel with a friend. I am well-acquainted with my own good intentions, but I judge my friend's actions in terms of their negative effects, thereby ignoring the point of view through which her intentions make sense as being directed to some good. The result is that I misunderstand and blame her. I fail to enter into her point of view, to appreciate that what she intended seemed good *to her*. Therefore, to understand someone's desire from their point of view, it is necessary to see what they intended or wanted as good, according to the phenomenologically appropriate descriptions.

Of course, this thesis doesn't mean that one should condone the other person's action or intention! Neither does it imply that their intention is all things considered good. One can distinguish between a) 'X is good/ desirable' and b) 'X is conclusively good/desirable, *all things considered*'. Nevertheless, the thesis does mean that there is some description of a person's intention that reveals it as directed towards something desirable. To understand another person well, it is necessary to characterise their desires or intentions in such terms.

Does the thesis imply that there is no such thing as a bad intention? No! It doesn't prohibit us from describing a person's intentions as bad. For example, we can still characterise them as selfish, harmful, and inhumane. However, these descriptions would be secondary or derivative because the thesis does imply that, to understand someone well, one must not characterise their intention as *primarily,* or in the first place as, directed towards something bad. The idea that some people are fundamentally evil depends on ignoring this point. In its extreme form, this can constitute demonising others.

The thesis has an important corollary – namely, that one tends to assume that one understands another person better than he or she understands oneself. In other words, there is a tendency to judge that I comprehend another person better than he/she understands me. This is a consequence of the main thesis because the epistemological asymmetry tends to portray any interaction as follows: I have access to his/her behaviour, but he/she doesn't have access to my intentions! The corollary is a consequence of the asymmetry of the first-person perspective. It embodies the same epistemological double-standard.

The corollary has yet another devastating implication – namely, that one tends to systematically underestimate the differences between oneself and another. If I have a propensity to think that I understand other people better than they understand me, then I will also be disposed to underestimate the differences between us. This is because I am trying to understand them only on my terms and not on theirs.

These epistemological limitations in understanding others constitute a form of systemic ignorance. Worse still, they are enhanced by the self-reinforcing nature of ignorance. It is the general nature of ignorance that one is predisposed to not know that one is ignorant. One tends to be ignorant of one's ignorance. Ignorance is like that: it doesn't know itself.

Here is a summary of the principles elucidated so far:

A. We tend to judge ourselves by our good intentions and others by the results of their actions;

B. We tend to assume that we understand others better than they understand us and underestimate the differences;

C. We tend to be ignorant of our ignorance of others;

D. Intentions are always directed primarily towards some perceived good.

We now need to see how these principles play out in group interactions. Because we are essentially social beings, we live in groups, and this means that we have affiliations and allegiances. This implies that we tend to identify with some groups and, in so doing, we don't identify with some other groups. In other words, identity is necessarily exclusionary. It is a question of 'us and them'. The 'them' gets excluded.

When we combine this point about identity with the four principles outlined above, we obtain a recipe for mutual misunderstanding and ignorance, for non-peaceful conflict.

Concerning the first principle, when we identify with a group, we tend to understand the good that we as a group intend, and ignore the good that the other group intends. We will tend to judge them by the results of their actions. The personal epistemological asymmetry tends to become socialised between groups, and, as such, tends to become solidified. This is part of what we mean when we say 'we identify' with a group, and not with others. We thereby exclude. The declaration 'this is my identity' can be akin to an affirmation of allegiance – that is, to perceive relevant situations in a group's way, which excludes perceiving them in the ways of the opposition groups (or the invisible groups). In short, we tacitly declare: "*We* intended to do good, but *they* did something bad." What starts off as exclusion becomes a tendency to think of some as the good guys and others as the bad guys.

The second principle (i.e., b) magnifies this effect. Extending the asymmetry, we tend to assume that other groups do not understand us (or at least not as well as we understand them). This can become the grounds for attributing bad intentions to the other group: "They don't understand us because they don't want to." This can develop over time into a fully-fledged grievance, which the other group, in turn, perceives as a hostility, and which fuels a vicious cycle of imputing negative intentions between the groups. Alfred Schutz elaborates this point when he claims that the in-group takes its interpretations of the world for granted, as a given, as if it were a part of nature. In contrast, the out-group does not hold these interpretations as self-evident. As a result, the in-group will feel that the out-group's failure to understand its way of life, "is rooted in hostile prejudice and bad faith" because the in-group assumes that its own interpretations are self-evident. The out-group will sense that the in-group perceives them with hostility, and a cycle of misinterpretation is established.[122] This dynamic is also enhanced by the fact that the in-group tends to underestimate the differences between itself and the other groups.

The third principle (i.e., c) shows us that we may be utterly unaware that this is happening and quite ignorant of our own ignorance of the other. Given this second-order ignorance, we tend to portray the situation as a natural condition, rather than as the result of a failed hermeneutic.

In sum, we have characterised some dynamics by which a group that starts off as 'an other' becomes, by degrees, transformed into an enemy. Now, juxtapose this with the fourth principle (i.e., d) that all intentions must be for some good. This applies to the intentions of our worst enemy, or the apparently most *evil* group. There is some description of even those persons' intentions that makes sense of their actions in terms of some good, and it is possible that we could also recognise it as such. This doesn't mean that we must agree with the person's judgments, but it does imply that we should acknowledge that there is some description of the situation that could be seen as good. In short, we should recognise that we could step into the shoes of even our worst enemy. This is implied by the claim that his/her point of view makes sense to him/her in a public language.

Recognition of this point embodies a fundamental ethical principle, which is that other people are equally as real as oneself and that no individual human life is intrinsically more valuable than any other. When we fall prey to epistemological asymmetry, and fail to attempt to see the good in what others will or desire, then we contradict this fundamental ethical principle. In effect, we succumb to the epistemological asymmetry, which is an offshoot of the childish illusion that 'I am more real and more important than others'. It is a kind of hermeneutical egoism that amounts to an unwillingness or incapacity to try to see the situation from the point of view of the other.

We can conclude that we have ethical obligations regarding how we construct our understanding of other people, especially those with whom we are in conflict. Ethically, we must be guided by the principle that all people are equally real. Epistemologically, we need to be led by the idea that others aim for the good too. Hermeneutically, we ought to be driven by the desire to overcome the afflictions of the asymmetries described earlier.

Usually, the prelude to overt violent conflict is a cultural and psychological violence that portrays the other as an enemy. This psychology is characterised by subjectivities that embody the asymmetries mentioned earlier, and which develops into a political culture of violence characterised as follows. Some groups are implicitly portrayed as less important than others, and the others as better and more important. As these portrayals become increasingly explicit, some groups are painted as lacking good intentions, with the implicit idea that they are evil. This is a prelude to depicting these other groups as less than human or sub-human.[123] Such dynamics may be motivated by and intertwined with material interests.

In practice, these dynamics mean that we need to deconstruct our conception of the other as an enemy. The popular portrayals of the other are non-peaceful constructions that can and need to be reversed. They need to be reversed because they contradict the fundamental ethical principle that we are all equals. They can be turned around because they are the cumulative effect of a history based on epistemological asymmetries. This deconstruction can be a long psychological and therapeutic process. However, there are ways or methods to help those who are willing to undertake such a deconstruction.[124]

HERMENEUTICAL DIALOGUE

The previous section indicates the primary importance of hermeneutic dialogue. Such dialogue requires the willingness to enter into the subjectivity of someone who one might be considered as an enemy, or as 'an other'. It aims at 'the fusion of horizons' as described by Gadamer.[125] The dialogue is hermeneutical because, to understand someone well, one must let the other challenge one's own assumptions, which requires confronting the relevant epistemological asymmetries and taking seriously the idea that all intentions aim at some good. Such dialogues typically involve a sharing that requires the willingness to listen to each other non-judgmentally and openly. In this section, I will make three points about such dialogues.

First, they are valuable in themselves. In the context of post-conflict situations, people working in the field of reconciliation are tempted to see hermeneutic dialogues, or workshops in which people share their experiences and trauma, merely as a means towards social healing and societal reconstruction. They are therapy. In pre-war conditions, one also is tempted to perceive such dialogues mainly as means to help de-escalate the build-up towards war or violence. They are preventative. In both cases, the groups talk to each mostly as a means to an end.

Given the ethical and epistemological importance of the asymmetry that we described earlier, we can appreciate the importance of hermeneutic dialogue as *a part* of being in peaceful relationships. Thus, such dialogues are not merely a means to avoiding violent conflict and to rebuilding social relations afterwards. They are not merely instrumentally valuable. They are also intrinsically valuable as part of what understanding others well signifies and what it means to live peacefully in a community. In short, such dialogues for their own sake are a part of living peacefully. In this way, they are more akin to an aspect of healthy living and less like taking pills before and after an operation. They are non-instrumentally valuable because they are a constitutive aspect of peaceful relations.

Second, hermeneutic dialogue contains an implicit commitment to the equal value of all persons as such, which enjoins us not to exclude or discount some people on the basis of their group identity. The non-instrumental value of such dialogue expresses certain ideals of equality. These ideals must include the equality of quality of listening: that all groups should be listened to with equal quality. To accept that we are equals, one must be willing to take up the point of view of the other. Insofar as one is not so willing, this indicates that one has effectively abandoned or suspended the ethical principle that all people are equally real, and that we are treating the epistemological asymmetry of egoism as a given. Given this, and that those who feel their voice has not been heard will resort to violence, some kinds of violence constitute a failure of the ideals of democratic dialogue. Violence is often the last resort of those who feel that they have not been listened to. Thus, in this sense, violence is the failure of dialogue.

Third, peace requires the idea that we transcend the dichotomy between victim and aggressor.[126] Following on from the epistemological asymmetries mentioned earlier, people and groups will always be prone to perceive themselves as victims, and see their relevant others (the enemy) as aggressors. This tendency is built within a combination of two factors: the subjectivity of our experience and our tendency to identify. It would be difficult to perceive ourselves, and the groups that we identify with as aggressors and the others with whom we don't identity as victims.

When, as a group, we identify ourselves as victims, this automatically means that we have grievances against the others whom we see as aggressors. We see how *we* have been hurt or humiliated by the others. We see how we have been denigrated and badly treated in the past. We simply assume that the other is an aggressor who has bad primary intentions. These are the kinds of subjectivity, both individual and collective, that render conflictual relations non-peaceful. In other words, peacefulness requires transcending subjectivities that are defined in terms of victim and aggressor.

These three points help us to define better what hermeneutic dialogue is. Such dialogue or sharing provides the opportunity for persons to transcend the subjectivities of oneself as victim and the other as aggressor. It allows us to understand how significant others perceive the relevant situations such that they see themselves as willing the good. It permits us to enter into the phenomenological reality of their point of view. In this sense, it consists in the attempt to listen without intentional pre-judgment and prejudice. It is defined by the qualities of good listening.

While these points help to define 'hermeneutic dialogue', in this section we also introduced an important idea – namely, that such dialogue isn't valuable purely in terms of its instrumentality in preventing violent conflict or restoring social relations after violent conflict. It is also something valuable in itself. It is a necessary feature of peaceful social relations.

A CRITIQUE OF JUST WAR THEORY

So far, we have argued that, because all persons are equal, we need to transcend epistemological, egoistic lopsidedness, and this requires that we recognise that others primarily will or intend good, just as one does oneself. We also claimed that peacefulness requires hermeneutic dialogues that overcome this epistemological skewedness as valuable in themselves, as an expression of equality. In this section, we shall argue that Just War Theory negates these broad principles. Just War Theory makes assumptions that are antithetical to the idea of a political culture of peace because the theory is radically incomplete.

Any theory is an attempt to respond to a set of questions. But every interrogation has a built-in set of assumptions that may need to be challenged. A query based on mistaken assumptions will yield misleading answers. I shall argue that Just War Theory fits this category. It is an attempt to answer questions based on erroneous assumptions. I will examine three flawed assumptions latent in the question, which constitute an impediment to a political culture of peace.

First, the theory asks the question, 'Is this war just?' from the perspective of a particular group. It is like asking: 'Are *we* (as a group or nation state) justified in waging war?' or, 'Do *we* have the right to fight?' The theory assumes the perspective of a country and asks from that point of view, 'Are *we* justified in retaliation?' or, 'Are we, as a country or group in these conditions and circumstances, justified in going to war?' Such questions assume the standpoint of a specific group. In other words, it is not taking a wider perspective, and it is not asking from that broader viewpoint, 'Is this war justifiable?'[127]

However, it is from the broader perspective that we can judge that war is a terrible form of insanity that is unjustifiable and should be prevented. Affirming this doesn't deny that war may look sane and rational from the narrower perspective of a group or nation who feel that they have no other option given their history, and given the actions of their enemy neighbour.[128] Despite this, the political culture of peacefulness will begin from the wider outlook, and, from there, include the perspectives of the combatants. In short, Just War Theory is misleadingly incomplete in the questions it tries to answer in that it ignores the wider perspective. Peacefulness requires us to adopt that broader view and inquire what such a view requires of an international political structure. It will ask positively, 'What must the international community do to become more peaceful?' Clearly part of the answer will include establishing institutional arrangements that help prevent forms of insanity appearing as rational from a narrow perspective.

Additionally, Just War Theory usually frames the issue in terms of the right of a country to go to war. It assumes a rights-based understanding of ethics or morality. In other words, it asks: 'Am I allowed to do this?' Such theories regard morality as a set of external constraints that an understanding of what is right imposes upon actions that we would otherwise want to perform in our own self-interest. This very way of framing moral questions subverts our understanding of a political culture of peacefulness as a positive value because it simply assumes that each group or nation will adopt a narrow self-interested view that is blind to the subjectivities of the other. It turns a question about a positive value into a query about how to restrain a negative.

The second assumption is that the question ignores the distinction between, on the one hand, issues concerning the morality of individual choice and actions and, on the other hand, questions about the morality of political systems and their resultant cultures. This distinction is vital. We need to distinguish:

A. Given framework F, or socio-political structure S, what is the morally right action in these circumstances?

B. Is framework F, or socio-political structure S, morally justifiable?

For example, questions about how a teacher should teach a class are different in kind from those that challenge the nature of the school as an institution and the educational system as a whole. The questions about how an individual should behave and choose within a given framework do not answer those concerning the framework itself. For instance, 'What is a good lesson plan for this part of the curriculum?' is an individual choice question that doesn't address issues regarding the framework, such as the design of the curriculum, its overall purposes, and their place within a society.[129] Likewise, explorations regarding how businesses should behave ethically don't serve to illuminate the issues concerning how the role of businesses should be defined within a political-economic framework.[130]

In a similar vein, the political culture of peacefulness needn't be committed to answering questions from within a framework that fundamentally needs revision. The conception of peacefulness needs to address the framework itself. 'When the framework is wrong, what should we do?' is an entirely different question from, 'Is the framework good?'[131]

Given this, it would be a mistake to try to define international political peacefulness solely in reaction to the question answered by Just War Theory, namely, 'When is a country justified in going to war?' Those who see war as justifiable tend to think in terms of the individual atomistic choices of nations, rather than seeing conflict as a systemic issue. For instance, they argue from a hypothetical example in which a family member would be violated by an intruder unless one acts violently. In such a situation, does one have the right to use violence? They answer,

'Of course, yes'. From this, they conclude that pacifism is mistaken and war is justifiable. However, the analogy is misleading. First, it seduces us into conflating emergency surgery and long-term prevention. Second, it disguises the relational nature of the term 'justified'. It frames the issue as only a matter of individual choice, without addressing political structural issues. Peacefulness as a positive value is committed to a world order in which peaceful relations reign.

This point is central because many aspects of the political culture of war depend on the fundamental assumption that war can be justifiable atomistically. As an advocate for peace, one might want to critically analyse many aspects of our violent political culture such as: war monuments; the language of the press; the transactions of the armaments industry; foreign policy rhetoric; militant patriotism, and the conception of retribution. Even the narratives of national history are 'weapons of mass instruction'. Sometimes, it seems that the whole edifice is constructed to make mass killing appear morally acceptable. However, this huge tower of institutions, industries, economic transactions, ideology, language, and ideas is based on a faulty assumption – namely, that war is justifiable as an individual nation's choice, but ignoring structural issues. We have argued that this conception of justifiable war is erroneous because it assumes that all moral questions can be reduced to the atomistic decisions of individuals.

The third assumption: When people ask the questions that Just War Theory is supposed to answer, they typically ignore the temporal framework. Usually, the question assumes a short temporal scope that would make an act of war look inevitable. As an analogy, if I drive unwisely, I may propel myself into the situation that makes it look inevitable that I must crash my car into a wall (to avoid something even worse). But something is unavoidable only with respect to a set of givens. I didn't need to drive myself into those circumstances of tragic inevitability. Thus, from a wider perspective, I don't need to treat those conditions as a given.

Likewise, even if war looks inevitable from a short-term perspective, this is so only given a set of assumptions about given circumstances that weren't inevitable. For instance, from the viewpoint of 1913, World War I might look inevitable. Likewise, given Versailles, World War II seems unavoidable.

Take a broader temporal view though and, suddenly, the whole dynamic looks very contingent. Europe could have avoided both wars.

To understand the build-up to a conflict, a long-term view is necessary. All violent conflicts seem to have roots in the more distant past. However, it isn't just that events, such as the battle of Karbala in 680 marked the differences between the Shia and Sunni, or the battle of Kosovo in 1389 helped to define the recent Balkans crisis. It is also necessary to apply the understanding of non-peaceful relations, and the ethics of hermeneutical dialogue to this long-term perspective.

Just War Theory thrives on the short-term perspective. But violent conflict draws its sustenance from long-term grievances. Just War Theory looks plausible only by assuming a short-term view of long-term problems or conflicts. Short-term thinking emphasises inevitability; long-term thinking emphasises contingency.

This problematic is accentuated by a misplaced ontology. The judgment that we are justified in waging war assumes a short-term perspective that sees history as a series of discrete events. The longer-term perspective sees history as a coalescence of distinct processes. The kind of historical understanding that we need for understanding peacefulness requires an ontology of processes, rather than one of atomistic events. There is a long-term set of processes that define the identity of group A, in part, in terms of a set of grievances against group B, and that mark event E as having a significance, given these antagonistic identities.

I introduced the idea of a 'just war' because there is a popular conception that defines peace as an absence of violent conflict, and which thereby misunderstands what peacefulness is. This conception is exemplified in Just War Theory, which attempts to answer questions that are limited or flawed in the assumptions they make. Likewise, pacifism, as the straightforward negation of the theory, falls prey to the same errors. To understand peacefulness, we need to reframe the questions and issues.

Because of this, there are some positive instructions to be drawn from rejecting Just War Theory. These are: first, peacefulness requires that we cannot approach war only from the perspective of a specific group. We need an impersonal perspective. Second, peaceful relations cannot be understood only from an atomistic ontology of individual choices from within given institutions and their frameworks. Peacefulness requires a systemic perspective. Thirdly, to understand what constitutes peaceful relations necessitates a long-term historical perspective that is process- rather than merely event-oriented.

Beyond these three specific lessons, there is a broader message. This is that violent conflict and war ought to be regarded as something morally unacceptable. It is a form of madness made possible by an atomistic framework. A political culture of peacefulness would not accept that frame. It would address itself primarily to the broader structural question, 'What does the positive value of peacefulness mean for international governance?' Among other things, the response would make it culturally impossible to regard violent action as a solution to problems that could in principle be avoided through institutions of peacefulness.

PEACEFUL POLITICAL SYSTEMS

What does it take for a systemic political organisation to be peaceful? The aim of this concluding section is to outline some of the principles necessary for the transition from individual hermeneutics to the structural. As we said earlier, even if peace is a spiritual condition, it is such that it must manifest itself as social relations, which will include the structural.

First, we need institutions at all levels that embody the principles articulated earlier in this paper. The purpose of section one of this paper was to describe the epistemological asymmetries that plague group identities. Given that these asymmetries are characteristic of the human condition, and, given the ethical principle of equality, we need socio-political institutions that enable us to overcome our tendency towards partiality, or hermeneutic egoism. For a person to embody peacefulness in her relations, it is necessary that she transcends the partial nature of these epistemological asymmetries, and, in so doing, respect that we are equally real, regardless of identities and social affiliations.

Second, we need institutional spaces for hermeneutic dialogues, as outlined in section two. Currently such dialogues tend to suffer from the shortcoming that they are conceived mainly as a remedy, or prevention of violence, and not as an integral part of peaceful relations. If a socio-political system were peaceful, then such dialogues would be part and parcel of its structure. How can people live in peace if they don't listen to each other? How can we listen to each other if there aren't suitably structured institutional spaces for listening? How can we know how marginalised groups feel in our community without spaces for sharing?

Third, we need institutions that build peace from a long-term, process-oriented approach to historical understanding. Clearly, the press tends to advocate an ontology based on short-term comprehension of atomistically conceived events. This popular view tends to emphasise events as atoms as opposed to historical processes.

The discussion in section three was intended to indicate the need for hermeneutical dialogues at the international level. In conclusion, politically, we need institutions that make such dialogues possible as non-instrumentally valuable processes.

122. Alfred Schutz, 1976, *Collected Papers* Vol. II, The Hague: Martinus Nijhoff, 53-56 and 243-248.

123. David Livingstone Smith, 2011, *Less than Human*, New York: St. Martin's Press.

124. Leonel Narvaez and Jairo Diaz, Edited by Leonel Narvaez, 2010, *Political Culture of Forgiveness and Reconciliation,* 'General Principle of Forgiveness and Reconciliation' and 'The Intellectual Autobiography of the Schools of Forgiveness and Reconciliation' Bogota, Fundación para la Reconciliación, 171-220 and 221-280.

125. Hans Georg Gadamer, 2006, *Truth and Method*, New York: Continuum Press.

126. I would like to thank Alexandra Asseilly and Leonel Narvaez for this understanding.

127. In this way, the claim 'X is justifiable' is ambiguous.

128. See John Lango, 2014, *The Ethics of Armed Conflict: A Cosmopolitan Just War Theory*, Edinburgh: Edinburgh University Press, Chapter 9.

129. For an example of this distinction at work, see Scherto Gill and Garrett Thomson, 2012, *Rethinking Secondary Education: A Human Centred Approach*, Oxford: Pearson.

130. This distinction is discussed in Garrett Thomson, Edited by Scherto Gill and David Cadman, *Why Love Matters*, 'Compassionate Governance in Corporations', Bern: Peter Lang, 79-92.

131. While the two are not entirely independent, the question 'Given where we are now, is nation X justified in waging war with nation Y?' is different from the question, 'From an impersonal long-term perspective, is war justifiable?' The answer to the second need not prejudice the answer to the first.

CHAPTER **EIGHT**

POSITIVE PEACE, SYSTEMS THINKING AND THE PROBLEMS OF OUR AGE

STEVE KILLELEA

PEACE IS TRANSFORMATIONAL. IF WE consider the people who have most inspired humanity throughout the ages – the great figures like the Buddha, Mahatma Gandhi and Jesus Christ – they had messages of peace that shook their ages and have remained with us ever since. In more recent times, the worldwide admiration felt for Nelson Mandela was in large part due to his prosecution of peace and forgiveness in post-apartheid South Africa. The great peacemakers attract attention because they change our world, while inspiring us to become more civilised and better human beings. And yet the way in which peace transforms is often imperceptible. What we tend to notice instead is its opposite, violence, and peace is typically understood in negative terms, as the absence of violence, or the fear of violence. Peace may be one of the most important elements for human flourishing, but the catch is that we are often not especially conscious of its existence, only its absence.

Looking at the dominant challenges facing humanity today, such as climate change, decreasing biodiversity, over-population and the availability of fresh water on the planet, just to name a few, it quickly becomes evident that, unless we create a world that is fundamentally peaceful, we will never achieve the levels of trust, cooperation and inclusiveness necessary to solve our problems. Therefore, peace has become a prerequisite for the survival of society as we know it in the twenty-first century, and this is different from any other epoch in human history. In the past, peace may have been the domain of the altruistic, but, in the twenty-first century, it's in everyone's self-interest.

There is an urgent need for peace, not least because, peace is especially pronounced in state-to-state relations. The development of advanced weaponry, especially nuclear bombs that can destroy the planet many times over, has highlighted the urgency of the need to maintain peaceful relations between nations. Likewise, the advancement in small arms and explosives means that even small forces can wreak havoc.

This new age is one in which, by necessity, humanity must now shape, sculpt and manage its environment. We must be the architect of biodiversity and the natural systems upon which we depend. If humanity is to survive and flourish, we need to find a way to live with Nature, rather than exploit Nature. As systems theory shows us, change is non-linear and, unless we continue to seek ways to live in harmony with Nature, our ever-compounding the problem will bring us to a tipping point. The tipping point, once passed, will be a profoundly disturbing epoch and one that we will not be able to backtrack from. Needless to say, a positive change of global proportions must be set in place.

MEASURING PEACEFULNESS AS A WAY TO PROMOTE PEACE

'Positive Peace' presents a new way of conceptualising peace. It is borne out of studying highly peaceful societies and it is a systemic approach to both building peace in the world and developing thriving societies.[132] It provides higher levels of sustainability and adaptability – the key to positively managing change. In more artificial man-made systems, there is a much greater requirement for self-examination to determine the consequences of actions. Put another way, instead of Nature being the adversary, the adversary increasingly becomes our own natures. We are required to peer into the mirror, to confront our own darker tendencies towards violence, selfishness and greed. In order to develop systems that will not eventually undo us, we will have to find new ways of being which effectively help us to live in harmony with ourselves, in our societies and with Nature.

A crucial part of developing such global self-awareness is the need to have sound measurements of human affairs. This is becoming essential to designing our future in the twenty-first century. Just as nautical maps were to the discovery of the New World in the sixteenth century, increasingly, we understand the world through examining and evaluating a vast span of human activity: economic growth, all types of transactions, trade flows, financial flows, crime rates, investment patterns, the incidence of disease, population trends, business activity, corruption, happiness and educational performance, to name just a few. Indeed, managing GDP growth is one of the chief ambitions of politicians and governments, shaping many of their policy decisions. It may be only a record of transactions, but it is becoming critically important in shaping behaviour. But, even as GDP becomes our chief yardstick of success, it is failing. How can GDP growth be successful when the living standards of large portions of the workforce are falling, or there is no recognition of the national capital account? The importance of measurement can also be seen in the ubiquitous polling in modern democracies of voters' attitudes. So powerful has this continuous number-gathering become, most political parties increasingly do their polling first to gauge the public's sentiment and only then set their political agenda.

This growing reliance on measurement has considerably increased our understanding of, and our ability to influence, the world. However, it does have profound limitations; one is the danger of exclusion – believing that only what can be measured exists and that only what is measured is important. This is patently false: you cannot measure the power of a Van Gogh painting, the sublimity of a Mozart concerto, or the beauty of a breaking wave, but that does not mean they do not exist. In the past, peace was seen in this light, only understood by the absence of something else – violence. Positive Peace challenges this and looks at peacefulness in and of itself.

POSITIVE PEACE

Expanding the boundaries of what can be measured is thus critical, especially for the things that matter, such as peace. Of equal importance is that these measures are acted upon, having a society focused on the things that really matter and understanding how these things are performing.

Peace is at the heart of social progress and what creates a peaceful society also creates the environment in which many of the other ideals to which we aspire can thrive. In its search for peace, the Institute for Economics and Peace studied highly peaceful societies to understand the most significant factors associated with these highly peaceful nations –Positive Peace. This is *the attitudes institutions and structures* that create and sustain peaceful societies, but it is much more than that as these same factors are also statistically associated with many other aspects that society considers desirable. Therefore, Positive Peace can be seen as creating an optimal environment for human potential to flourish.

Although measuring Positive Peace is of great importance for the destiny of the human race, there are limitations when identifying it directly. Comparatively, measuring violence can be done directly by looking at acts of violence, or measuring people's fear of violence, whereas Positive Peace can only be seen in outline by looking at what affects it. It is not directly observable in itself. It is a bit like measuring gravity. Nobody doubts the existence of gravity. Any child sitting on a balcony knows that it is real, but gravity cannot be seen or touched, nor can it be observed under microscopes or telescopes.

In the seventeenth century Isaac Newton formulated his Universal Law of Gravitation in the *Principia Mathematica*. He proposed that gravity was one of the central forces in the universe, which seemed to settle many of the outstanding scientific dilemmas of his time. However, two centuries later, Albert Einstein, while working as a patent clerk in Switzerland, theorised that gravity is not something that can be isolated and measured, like a star or an electrical current. Instead, he believed, it is the curve of space itself, inherent in the very geometry of space and time. Peace in human affairs is somewhat similar. It cannot be directly observed, it can only be discovered by inference. No reasonable person doubts that peace is real, or denies its importance, but what creates peace cannot be detected in the same direct way as specific human acts, as it is a collective, background act, something systematic.

The Global Peace Index provides a starting point as it measures the levels of violence, or fear of violence, for 162 countries, or 99.5 percent of the world's population. It can then be used to statistically derive what factors are most commonly associated with peaceful societies. The outcome of this is then used to cluster the most statistically significant results together, forming a topology of eight factors called the Pillars of Peace (see Figure 1). The number of Pillars is a balancing act and there cannot be too many categories because this then becomes unintelligible – and, therefore, of little use. These eight Pillars can be seen as highly interconnected and interacting in varied and complex ways to form either virtuous or vicious cycles.

Figure 1: Pillars of Peace (Source: Institute for Economics and Peace)

The strength of the various interactions between the different Pillars of Peace will depend on the historical, political, economic, and cultural circumstances of particular societies. However, without knowing what those Pillars of Peace are and having some way of measuring them, it is not possible to gain a sound understanding of a country's peacefulness. This is the essence of systems thinking, where there is an analogy with health. It is generally accepted that the human body acts as a system. If you are studying a disease, then you focus on the part of the body where it is occurring and address that particular area. Analysing negative peace is like looking at a disease – you only focus on where the violence is occurring and its consequences. If you are studying wellness, however, you look at all parts of the body, trying to work out how they might interrelate and interact in order to promote good health, which, in turn, prevents disease from occurring. The interactions will vary from individual to individual, but achieving a holistic picture will lead to a wider understanding of what constitutes good health.

The measures of Positive Peace are complex and systematic. As a simple example, if there is an increase in the incidence and perception of corruption, this will undoubtedly have an effect on business, the functioning of government, and the free flow of information. But changes in corruption may also be partly caused by those very same variables. Likewise, actions have systemic consequences; many things can function in a non-linear and lagged way. It is not possible to say that when certain attributes reach a certain level, we will see violence – rather, what we can say is that when one variable deteriorates, others are likely to as well. Together, these dynamics cause community stress and build up the grievances that make violence more likely. An example was the Arab Spring; it started with one Tunisian street vendor setting himself on fire. The tipping point is difficult to see, but the background context can be understood. But even when we can see the general context, it does not provide the ability to predict with certainty.

Positive Peace tends to move slowly and large changes tend to occur over decades, rather than years. This is not the case with negative peace, which can deteriorate comparatively quickly if there is a sudden increase in violence and can improve quickly, if, for instance, a civil war finishes.

Positive Peace includes both formal and informal societal factors; societal and attitudinal factors are as important as state institutions. In countries where capacity is lacking in formal institutions, informal processes may fill the void. For instance, tribal justice and tribal courts are often more trusted by communities than the national judicial systems in parts of Africa. Many such informal institutions are ongoing and can be conducted in partnership with formal institutions.

An example of this was the genocide in Rwanda in 1994. The judicial system did not have the capacity to deal with the large number of cases, which the courts acknowledged. There were too many cases and the system had deteriorated because of the genocide, where many of its ranked officials were killed. So the government agreed to set up traditional community Gacaca courts: grassroots courts. Not all the results were sound – there are both good and bad stories attached to these courts – but they tackled as many as two million cases and are often heralded as one of the reasons Rwanda has not fallen into even deeper entrenched violence.[133] It also created vital time to build up much needed capacity in the official judicial system.

Positive Peace also builds the capacity for societal resilience and the possibility and incentives for nonviolent alternatives in terms of conflict resolution. Stronger Positive Peace reduces the level of violence within a society in many ways. It provides a much more resilient system as it removes the source of grievances that could generate violence, and it means that legitimate and effective nonviolent resolution avenues are on offer. A decrease in violence will also lead to a virtuous cycle. Less is spent on violence containment, allowing more funds in the future to divert into further reinvestment in Positive Peace, thereby building capacity and making reductions in future violence. Conversely, a deterioration in Positive Peace can reveal how potentially fragile a country is.

POLITICS AND PEACE

If we accept that finding a path towards a sustainable planet is critical for the survival of the human race, then peace is the bedrock on which it must be built. However, the mere measurement of peace alone is insufficient. The challenge is to develop a shared understanding, one that accounts for our interdependence within the broader ecological system. This inevitably leads to a political discussion. Today's politics are plagued by self-interest, nationalist jingoism, and a growing level of apathy among the citizens of many countries, particularly the developed Western nations. If ever there was a need for a global political movement that transcends national boundaries, it is now.

A global political movement would require the reexamination of our political thinking. The politics of the twenty-first century remain defined by notions of the left and right that were mainly derived from eighteenth- and nineteenth-century thinkers, such as Adam Smith, Karl Marx, and the Fabians. Many of these simple ways of pigeonholing are no longer applicable to the current state of the world. It is scarcely surprising that electorates are becoming increasingly disillusioned with major parties. The concept of a holistic approach is desperately required so that human potential can truly flourish. Positive Peace is both innately appealing and practically necessary.

For the last 300 years, Western nations have dominated and this was brought about by the combination of many factors, such as empiric scientific techniques, a focus on evolving more inclusive forms of government, and improved human capital. However, it would appear that Western advancement may have stalled because, although Positive Peace is improving in nearly all regions of the world, in many countries in Europe and the US, it is actually falling. In fact, the US has had one the largest falls in Positive Peace globally and this can now be seen playing out in its domestic politics.

The advanced Western democracies appear to be at turning point and, in the case of the US, it may be a tipping point. As political systems are captured more and more by money, particularly big business, the virtuous cycle that started at the end of World War II appears to have come to a standstill and, in some cases, such as the US, it has reversed. This, combined with global challenges, makes finding a new paradigm essential.

Therefore, to understand peace is not just to understand the political environment. It is to understand the *purpose* of politics in the postindustrial era. It is practically unheard of for politicians to promise to their electorates that they will create peace using positive methods. All too often, unfortunately, they tend to, instead, perpetuate fear, attempting to scare the electorate into voting for them. It is only when they leave politics that many of them start to become interested in working for peace, having realised the failures of the system.

The virtues of Positive Peace are multifaceted and improvements in Positive Peace create a greater capacity for resilience and adaptability. The higher the Positive Peace, the more likely nonviolent outcomes with concessions are made in society to reconcile grievances. For instance, countries with higher levels of Positive Peace, when faced with civil resistance movements, are much less likely to become violent. The movements typically have more limited aims, exist for a shorter period of time and are more likely to be successful in achieving concessions from the state. For countries experiencing major resistance campaigns, 91% of all violent resistance campaigns have been waged in countries with weaker Positive Peace. Countries with weaker Positive Peace are less able to recover and are less resilient in the face of civil resistance. In these countries, antagonistic movements tend to be larger, more violent, and have more radical aims, continuing for longer.

An example of a high Positive Peace country is Iceland. It also happens to be the most peaceful country in the world. It was the country most affected by the global financial crisis and it effectively became bankrupt after its banking system collapsed. However, there were only a few demonstrations and, within 12 months, a new political party was formed who won the election, created a government and then implemented major changes. Iceland restructured and was able to repay much of its debt to the IMF early. Contrast this to Greece which has lower levels of Positive Peace. Its financial crisis saw the rise of far-right parties associated with violence.

Where Positive Peace is stronger, better development outcomes ensue. Countries with higher levels of Positive Peace fared better in achieving their Millennium Development Goals than those with lower Positive Peace. Likewise, countries that are strong in Positive Peace also have better performing economies. Between 1996 and 2013, countries which improved in Positive Peace had a 1.6% higher per annum growth rate than countries that deteriorated, this again highlighting the interdependent nature of peace and other forms of flourishing.

Globalisation has delivered benefits and this can be seen by rising standards of the very poor in many parts of the world, resulting in a massive reduction of human misery. However, the benefits of globalisation in the developed world are less pronounced. The political parties which have historically been about delivering social equity have now become dominated by the politics of identity, especially as expressed in terms of gender equality and LGBT rights. Although these causes are in themselves worthy, they have come to dominate the values of the parties that once represented the poor. Often these values represent the values of liberal elites and have little connection with the bottom 25% of society who are struggling in a world where their job security and their income levels are falling and stress levels are rising.

Modern political campaigning is becoming more and more expensive as well. The source of the funds for electioneering mainly comes from companies or wealthy individuals. Many of these companies donate to both sides of politics – investing for their company's growth would be the way they see it. This trend seems to have no end in sight. The rise of popularism is a natural by-product of this alienation of the political elite and the upper middle class from the needs of ordinary people. The popularist movements will struggle to deliver what their voters want. Their policies mainly aim at channelling, arguably, justifiable anger towards immigrants and big political structures, such as the EU, or Muslim groups. None of these issues will solve the decaying living standards of the working class.

When looking at France, US, Australia, UK, and the Netherlands through some of the Positive Peace Pillars, it gives an insight into these changing dynamics. Gender rights have improved in all five countries over the last decade. However, measures of human rights have fallen in all these countries, except Australia, while group grievances have increased in all countries, except the Netherlands. When looking at equitable distribution of resources, the indicator for inequality-adjusted life expectancy has deteriorated in all. Corruption is another Positive Peace Pillar that has fallen in all countries, especially those governed by fractionalised elites, which is a measure of political tensions and political competition. In fact, the overall Positive Peace scores in all five countries have fallen. The US had the third largest fall in the last decade of any country in the world. The political upheaval we are witnessing is simply a by-product of the loss of Positive Peace. This group of countries can be contrasted to the rest of the world where two thirds have had an overall increase in their levels of Positive Peace.

The statistical picture is both holistic and concrete and shows that changes need to be made, but it is more than focusing on improving indicators. Fixing these problems is not easy; it requires a fundamental change in the way politics is conducted and the way society envisions itself. Ultimately, it is about the system: we need new ways of conceptualising societies and invigorating our institutions, with a focus on flourishing.

WE ARE PART OF THE SYSTEM

At the heart of a future sustainable world is the realisation that we are part of the system – we are not independent of it. One of the biggest illusions of Western philosophical thought is the concept of linear causality. The centrality of this in Western thought extends back to the Greeks, Parmenides and Aristotle, and, much later, this was used as the grounds for Newton's laws of thermodynamics. Matter cannot be created or destroyed, but it can be transformed through processes. This has been reinforced by the Western theological idealism: God stands immutable, perfect and unchanging, creating the universe and controlling the destiny of all, including humanity. The first cause from which all else sprang.

The concept of causality is inherent in our understanding of the world and the way we interact within it; it is built into our subconscious. We take an action and expect an outcome. Walk down a street and each footstep that we unconsciously take is attributable to a built-in understanding of cause and effect. In the physical world, actions have an effect which always results in the same outcome, such as gravity. Throw a ball into the air and it will always fall at the same rate. Ideas of cause and effect also appeal to us because they lead to the creation of apparently persuasive narratives or stories. Both stories and explanations of cause and effect are linear: a 'cause' is like the beginning of a story, an 'effect' is like the end of a story. The difficulty is that such an approach is partial and incomplete.

It is true that our understanding of the physical world through examining causality has enabled great strides in human progress. Modern empirical science arose because of it. But there are problems. Causality implies that all causes can be tracked back linearly to an initial condition. The logical extension is that we live in a clockwork universe where the conditions are predetermined and there is no room for genuine novelty. This stands in contradiction to our experience of reality. Causality is excellent for explaining discrete and isolated phenomena. But when multiple variables are involved, it becomes increasingly difficult to truly understand the cause.

It has led to the concept of causeless correlations, which is fundamental to systems thinking and forms the basis of how we think about Positive

Peace. An example would be the relation between the free flow of information and a well-functioning government. Governments can regulate what information is available, but information can also change government. The two are highly correlated, but both mutually affect each other. Where multiple variables interact, science has great difficulty in understanding their interactions, which makes it exceptionally difficult to map and understand highly complex systems. This is especially true for biological systems, such as human beings. It can be dangerous to apply scientific laws to human systems because, in human systems, the participants are aware of what is happening.

This leads to the conclusion that the universe is ultimately heading to sameness and disorganisation. The problem of using this to apply to Nature is that it is inadequate to explain living organisms, which increase in differentiation and also complexity, in other words, evolving in the opposite direction. Evolution is anti-entropic: it cannot be explained by looking at its pre-existing conditions and drawing quasi-scientific conclusions about causation.

The heavy emphasis on causality has also led to great specialisation. Subjects are broken down into smaller and smaller parts in order to find how their constituents work. It is difficult for many outsiders to understand specialisations. The terminology that is specific to these specialisations has proliferated, thereby hindering communication with the 'uninitiated'. This specialisation in many respects is problematic. When we look at the major challenges facing humanity in the twenty-first century, it is clear that there is an urgency to understand interdependence. Specialisation blocks our perception and ability to study and understand such relationships, many of which are vital to the future of humanity.

What I am proposing here is to consider systems thinking as a meaningful alternative to transforming our world. Applying systems thinking at the national level is revolutionary, changing the way we view societies, leading to whole new ways of conceptualising human development, the functioning of the state, and the role of individuals within it.

Today, most government decisions are based on understanding things through cause and effect. Do this, get that result, using the same stimulus in all situations. Causality ceases to be important in systems thinking; rather relationships, flows, momentum, and tipping points become the focus. New concepts arise to study countries, such as national intent and encoded norms. In the same way that individuals have an intent with their actions, so do nations. Encoded norms are the way a nation responds to an event. How do individuals or groups of individuals respond and what are government's reactions? These concepts apply both to conflict-affected countries, as well as the most advanced states. Positive Peace provides the lens from which to view and stimulate these national systems and sets in motion self-reinforcing actions that sustain and improve our societies. This offers a new way of conceptualising our approach to survival and how to flourish.

Systems thinking can be applied to both the ways societies operate and is also commonly used in understanding the way ecosystems operate. Combined with Positive Peace, this provides a new way of envisioning our societies and their goals.

In understanding systems thinking, there are some very basic precepts which clearly differentiate it from cause and effect thinking.

- The system cannot be reduced to its parts without altering its pattern. This is the opposite of a brick wall, or a library which is only the sum of its parts.

- The system is homeostatic. In other words, it tries to maintain a stable state. A simple, but good example is the maintenance of body temperate. It stabilises itself through feedback loops. The system adjusts its outputs to create a match between its inputs and internally coded requirements. These encoded norms within a nation could be the response to eradicating a new infectious disease, or the maintenance of the electricity supply system.

- The system is self-organising and can modify itself. When there is a persistent mismatch between inputs and its codes, the system searches for a new pattern by which it can function. This creates differentiation from the original system and increases complexity.

- The system does not stand on its own. It is part of a larger system, but it also has its own identity with its own different set of codes. It is open to inputs from the larger system and there are subsystems contained within it and there are other similar systems. This hierarchy of systems adapts together. The more open the systems, the more inclusive are the structures or patterns. They will adapt together.

Systems thinking can be approached from many directions. One direction is to think of the system as an organisation, rather than a series of events. Put another way, what is important in systems is the flow and the patterns, rather than just events.

A system cannot be reduced to its component parts to fully understand it. This is self-evident as anyone reading this book would see themselves as being self-aware and conscious, which is much more than the sum of their parts. The nature or character of a system will be altered with the addition, subtraction or modification of any piece. If this does happen, the system will modify and change and bring into existence a new variation, which in some way will function differently than the original system. Once changed, it can never go back. The process is called path dependency because the way a system functions depends on its current trajectory (path) and it cannot stand independent of this. It is often said that the approach should be to nudge the system in the right direction, rather than dramatically redesigning it.

Focusing heavily on causality often results in missing the nuances, variations, and overarching patterns. This is simply because there is a tendency to assume that the same cause will lead to the same outcome. Consider a simple conversation: emphasising causality would imply that the same words should have the same effect on whoever they are spoken to. This is obviously incorrect. Imagine these words I have written here are read by three different people. Each will interpret them differently, depending on their background knowledge, what they may think of the writer, or perhaps even their mood on the day. Therefore, the actions of these three people, based on the same inputs, can be very different.

If individual human reactions can be so variable, imagine how much more complicated a social system is. Then extend it onto the international stage and consider the same actions occurring in different nations and how very different the outcomes may be. Imagine the same political speech in America, one given at a political rally, and the same speech given in North Korea. The reactions would be strikingly different because the cultural norms are so far apart. From a systems perspective, each casual factor does not need to be understood. The system is self-managing.

There is also a concept known as mutual feedback loops. Processes can be mutually causal. Factors such as corruption and business mutually affect each other and, as corruption increases or decreases, business reacts and changes its practices. These reactions can then further modify the way corruption is undertaken. Consider improvements in health services. This provides for a more productive workforce, which, in turn, provides the government with a higher income, whereby more money can then be invested back into health: hence there is mutual reciprocity between cause and effect. Think of two political parties too, always changing and reacting to the policies and actions of the other.

In systems thinking, things do not exist in isolation; they are mutually dependent on each other and other systems. Cells within the body depend on the health of the being, while the being depends on the health of the cells. Similarly, countries depend on the health of companies, the education system, and policing, as well as the health of the family and individuals. These can also be viewed as systems contained within the nation state. They are mutually interdependent and each will have their own intents and encoded norms. Think of the way a police department operates compared to a school: it has very different encoded norms. Such mutual dependency is part of the nature of a system, whether it's an ecosystem, atmospheric system, or a society. So it is with peace – to create peace, a whole range of positive factors must be in place.

Systems thinking also has tipping points and this makes it possible to understand how small catalytic events, which are separated by distance and time, can be the cause of significant, seemingly disproportionate changes. The fall of the Berlin Wall started with the loosening of the authoritarian state in the USSR, leading to demonstrations in East Germany that culminated in the joining of East and West Berlin. No one could have predicted this outcome. With peace, there are also tipping points. Two of particular note relate to a country's GDP and corruption. Per capita income does not increase by much until a certain level of peace is reached, after which small increases in peace are associated with big increases in per capita income. Equally, as corruption increases, there are only small changes in peace, but, once a certain point is reached, then small increases in corruption result in large decreases in peace. These effects are not only non-linear, they can also be lagged. Think of education: its real impact can be seen many years after graduation. The impact will increase as those who have been educated in new ways of thinking gain power, sometimes many decades after graduating from school.

CONCLUSION

We live in dangerous times, when nuclear weapons can destroy all life on the planet many times over, but equally as threatening is the gradual decay of the ecosystems with which humanity is codependent. Western democracies are faltering, stuck with encoded norms that clearly are becoming less effective. The politics of identity undermine the politics of compassion.

Changes need to be made, but it is about more than focusing on improving indicators – it's about the system, which not only helps provide new ways of understanding peace and perceiving our realities, but also enables us to reconceptualise global societies, redesign our institutions and, above all, recognise our interdependency. I believe that through the lenses of systems thinking, Positive Peace offers a holistic framework so that we might re-envision a future that we can all be part of, one in which all lives can thrive and flourish.

---

132. Here I refer to the Positive Framework developed by the Institute for Economics and Peace and the Global Peace Index, a comprehensive measurement of countries' peacefulness, launched in 2006.

133. P Clark, 2010, *The Gacaca Courts, Post-Genocide Justice and Reconciliation in Rwanda: Justice without Lawyers*, Cambridge: Cambridge University Press.

CHAPTER NINE

TOWARDS A PEACEFUL ECONOMY

STEWART WALLIS

WHEN I WAS THE DIRECTOR of the New Economics Foundation, I met with a fellow director of another economic think-tank. He said that the difference between my think-tank and his was that we practised values-based economics and they practised value-free economics. I laughed at him. There is no such thing as value-free economics – all economics is values-based. The problem is that the values are usually not made explicit. And, yet, the values based on which economies are organised are the crucial determinant of their outcomes for societies and the planet.

The current economic system is based on the idea that we are independent, rational individuals motivated primarily by wealth and success, and that, if everybody pursues their own selfish goals, then the well-being of society is maximised. This is not only a gross simplification of who we are as humans, but it is increasingly harmful. Indeed, arguably, the most pervasive and insidious form of violence affecting both our everyday lives and international conflict is the violence inherent in the neoliberal market economy.

This should come as no surprise since the root of such an economy is competition and consumption without limit. It is a system of abstractions; it lauds the individual over community; and it favours the rich over the poor. It often eschews regulation and law and its language is violent, such as the common use of expressions, such as 'takeover battles' and 'making a killing'. It does not seek justice or peacefulness, but rather wealth and power. There is connection, but not relationship.

If this was restricted to the buying and selling of vegetables, it might not matter much. But the language of the neoliberal market economy has come to pervade every part of our being. Hospitals, schools and old people's homes have been privatised so that they are brought within the rules of economy. Patients have become 'customers', or even 'service users'. A university vice chancellor was heard to tell the gathered professors that they had to 'sweat their assets', and a hospital nurse described a 'crisis' as having given treatment to a man who hadn't disclosed that he had no health insurance.

The neoliberal market economy has become so dominant that we have come to suppose that it is the only kind of economy that we could have, and that to resist it would be to bring society to its knees. None of this is true. And it is beset with paradox. Businesses start up and then fail all the time. That is surely inherent to the neoliberal market economy – no safety nets! How can it then be that some parts, especially the large international banks, are to be protected and subsidised? Is this not an irony?

DAMAGES OF A VIOLENT ECONOMY

What harm has this violent economy caused? Firstly, it has done massive harm to the planet and all creatures that live on the planet; secondly, it has caused huge injustices in the form of inequality and the severance of trust; thirdly, it has created insecurity for most people on the planet; and, fourthly, it has made many people feel insignificant and undervalued. To take each of these in turn:

PLANET: For the 200,000 years or so that we humans have lived on this planet, we have lived within its capacity to provide the resources we need and to process our wastes. Up to 40 years ago, that is. In the last 40 years, we've gone from using one planet's worth of resources each year to using one and a half, and we are on course to using three planet's worth by 2050.[134] Of course, we only have one planet, and the results of this overuse and abuse are plain to see. We are at serious risk of runaway climate change with dire consequences for humans and other creatures. Summer Arctic sea ice levels are only half of what they were 30 years ago in terms of area and a quarter of what they were in terms of volume. In 2016, temperatures in December at the North Pole were above freezing, which is unprecedented. Most of the planet's ecosystems – our life-support systems – are in decline or serious decline. This includes pollination systems, fish stocks, freshwater, coral reefs and air quality. Vertebrate species populations in the world are about half the size they were 40 years ago. We are seriously exceeding planetary limits in the nitrogen and phosphorus cycles and are on the verge of creating the first human-caused mass extinction.

INJUSTICE: We now have a situation where the eight richest individuals in the world have as much wealth as the poorest half of humanity – 3.5 billion individuals. In 2016, the 1% richest people in the world had more wealth than the other 99% for the first time. In the USA, the growth in income of the poorest 50% of the population has been zero over the last 30 years, whereas the incomes of the top 1% have grown 300%. In the UK, a FTSE-100 CEO earns as much in a year as 10,000 people working in garment factories in Bangladesh.[135] This level of inequality is totally unsustainable and is causing untold social harm. It is also leading to a breakdown of trust in most Western-style democracies. The 2017 Edelman Trust Barometer showed that most of the general population in those countries now believe the system is failing them – 53% said the system was failing them, 32% were uncertain and only 15% stated that the system was working. Trust has been lost in all the major institutions of society – government, businesses, public bodies, the media, banks, and non-governmental organisations.[136]

INSECURITY: There is widespread agreement in the richer countries of the world that the social contract is broken – especially the link between hard work and reward and security. Many people fear the loss of their jobs, insecurity in old age, and the destruction of their dreams and cultural norms. Globally, population increases and demographics mean that 50 million new jobs, or livelihoods need to be created every year between now and 2050[137] – at the same time, artificial intelligence experts are forecasting 25% global unemployment by 2050 unless the economic system is changed.[138] Our current economic system cannot provide full-time jobs for everybody (even if this was desirable) and the quest to do so will just cause irreparable harm to the planet. Even nine years after the crash of 2008/9, youth unemployment levels in Spain are at 44%. At the same time, public expenditure is being cut in many countries and austerity rules, so that many things that we have taken for granted would be provided by the state are now being cut. We are in a situation where neither the brake nor the accelerator work anymore in our economic system. If we try to put our foot harder on the accelerator, we burn up the planet even faster; if we put our foot on the brake, we cause greater inequality and unemployment. People intuitively know that the system is broken, even if they don't articulate this and, as a result, most people feel increasingly insecure.

INSIGNIFICANCE: As Sebastian Junger states in his new book *Tribe: On Homecoming and Belonging*, "Humans don't mind hardship, in fact, they thrive on it; what they mind is not feeling necessary. Modern society has perfected the art of making people not feel necessary. It's time for that to end."[139] So many people today feel that they have no voice and are of no value. As Aditya Chakraborty wrote in the *Guardian* recently:

A health worker in Pontypool told me what happens when people lose their sense of purpose. 'You don't get up in the morning. You might see a spiral in depression,' she said. 'You lose contact with the outside world.' The dismal list went on: no self-worth, no self-confidence [...] As she talked, I realised her description didn't apply only to people. Places and communities can be stripped of their purpose too. That is certainly what's happened to Pontypool." He goes on to say, "The story of Pontypool is a story of riches squandered, of dynamism blocked, of an entire community slung on the slagheap. Sat atop vast deposits of iron ore and coal, it was probably the first industrial town in Wales. For a time, under Victoria, it was richer than Cardiff. Swaths of Pontypool and the surrounding region of Torfaen now rank among the poorest in all Britain. On part of one of its housing estates in Trevethin, 75% of all children under four are raised in poverty. Over half, 53%, of all households who live on that stretch are below the poverty line. With that come all the usual problems: families that can't pay the rent, that are more likely to fall prey to a whole range of sicknesses, from mental health to cancer. Those people can expect to die 20 years before their near-neighbours in some of the better-off areas in Pontypool. First the economy died out, now its people are too."[140]

This was a major factor both in the Brexit vote and in the election of Donald Trump.

How on earth did we get to this situation where we have an economy that is causing so much harm?

THE ORIGIN OF OUR ECONOMIC SYSTEM

The current economic system was made by men, 36 of them. They met in 1947 at the Mont Pelerin hotel in Switzerland to build the intellectual basis of neoliberalism. They included Ludwig von Mises, Fredrich von Hayek, and Milton Friedman. They believed that government interference in the economy was totally wrong, and they had four key principles: individual freedom, free markets, small government and strong defence.

Initially, they managed to have a powerful influence on the teaching of economics, with the Chicago School being the most prominent example. However, by the late 1960s, they came to believe that their project was failing. In 1971, at the request of the head of the US Chamber of Commerce, Lewis Powell, soon to become a Supreme Court Justice, penned a strategy to promote the neoliberal project. On the strength of that document, a variety of foundations and donors committed millions of dollars to the creation and endowment of the organisations that would take the neoliberal principles previously found in academic circles and make them the dominant global economic narrative. These organisations included the Heritage Foundation, Cato Foundation, and the Institute for Economic Affairs. The rest is history. Thatcher and Reagan came to power at the end of the 1970s and made the neoliberal project a political reality. They cut the welfare state, took on the unions, lowered taxes dramatically, and privatised many public and mutual organisations and services.

Other economic models, such as Keynesian economics, which advocates the management of aggregate demand using public sector investment at times when private sector investment is slack, have at times had a powerful influence. However, they are no longer in favour, being seen as fettering the beneficial work of 'free markets'. Most recently, economists such as the Chicago School, have proposed and reified the notion of 'efficient markets', so that it has become almost heresy to see the market as anything other than free and perfect. It has certainly become heresy to suggest that markets need regulating. These models – and increasingly so – see economic growth based upon measures of GDP as the *sine qua non* of economic policy and wellbeing. 'Economic growth' has become today's political and economic mantra.

As Manfred Max Neef has said:

> The extraordinary thing about 19th century neo-classical economics is that it has achieved its final success in the late 20th century. This is amazing indeed. We no longer have a physics of the 19th century nor a 19th century biology or astronomy or geology or engineering. All sciences have shown a permanent evolution. Economics is the only discipline where problems of the 21st century are supposed to be interpreted, analysed and understood using 19th century theories.[141]

And, in all of this, it would seem, the further we move away from the real and physical, especially when we 'gear-up' our activities with debt, the more we find ourselves in an unstable, useless, and yet lucrative world of financial 'trading' and 'speculation'. There is an evident incompatibility between true physical wealth and debt-funded speculation, and a society based upon the latter is always fragile. It is only held together by the precarious convention of asset pricing, a world of virtual trades and speculations. And the enormity of this world is staggering. In 2013, it was calculated that this market of financial derivatives amounted to some $700 trillion, which was then more than ten times the GDP of the entire world, and equivalent to $100,000 for every single person in the world, men women and children – a time bomb waiting to explode with catastrophic consequences.

Steve Keen, Professor and Head of the School of Economics, History and Politics at Kingston University and the author of *Debunking Economics* has provided a sharp analysis. Drawing on the repeated global financial crises, he argues that our economic theory based on neoclassical economics is not merely wrong, but, more importantly, it is dangerous. The reason that neoclassical economics contributed directly to this crisis is that it promotes, "faith in the innate instability of a market economy, in a manner which in fact increased the tendency toward instability of the financial system."[142] Keen continues to explain:

> With its false belief that all instability in the system can be traced to interventions in the market, rather than the market itself, it championed the deregulation of finance and the

dramatic increase in income inequality. Its equilibrium vision of the functioning of finance markets led to the development of the very financial products that are now threatening the continued existence of capitalism itself.

Simultaneously it distracted economists from the obvious signs of an impending crisis – the asset market bubbles, and above all, the rising private debt that was financing them. Paradoxically, as capitalism's 'perfect storm' approached, neo-classical macro-economists were absorbed in smug self-congratulation over their apparent success in taming inflation and the trade cycle, in what they termed, "The Great Moderation."[143]

In 2015, a group of applied mathematicians released the Human and Nature Dynamical Study (HANDY)[144] warning that, "Cases of severe civilisational disruption due to precipitous collapse — often lasting centuries — have been quite common." The title, *Human And Nature Dynamical Study (HANDY): Is Industrial Civilization Headed for Irreversible Collapse?*, was clearly chosen for the acronym, but the subtitle crisply sets forth its thesis. Using a NASA-funded climate model, it explored the history of prior collapses to understand long-term human behaviour. It did not set out to make short-term predictions, but the warning is stark. The study described the collapses variably as: population decline; economic deterioration; intellectual regression and the disappearance of literacy (Roman collapse); serious collapse of political authority and socioeconomic progress (repeated Chinese collapses); disappearance of up to 90% of the population (Mayan), and some so complete that the forest swallowed any trace until archaeologists rediscovered what had been clearly complex societies (many Asian collapses).

The authors concluded that despite the common impression that societal collapse is rare, or even largely fictional, "the picture that emerges is of a process recurrent in history and global in its distribution."[145]

These collapses, they argued, were neither inevitable, nor natural; they were human-caused. Regardless, they inflict massive misery, often for centuries after. The study identified two underlying causes of collapse throughout human history: "... *the stretching of resources* due to the strain placed on ecological carrying capacity", and "... *the economic stratification of society* into Elites [rich] and Masses or 'Commoners' [poor]." These features, the study concluded, have played, "a central role in the process of the collapse" in all cases over "the last 5,000 years."[146]

For the first time in human history, these two underlying causes currently exist across the whole planet, rather than being confined to a geographic region. The risk that our violent economic system poses to ourselves and so many innocent species is obvious.

TOWARDS PEACEFUL ECONOMY

At the heart of the peaceful economy we want to build, there must be three core values: Human Dignity – which requires that people are not just valued, but feel valuable; Promotion of the Common Good – which can be defined as the creation of 'real value'; and Stewardship – of the planet and for future generations. Living these values will require us to shift how society views people and how we often view ourselves – a shift from consumers and owners to caretakers and creators. Values provide us a clear destination – a True North – and the motivation to get there.

A system based on these values would have the following goals:

First, it would meet the fundamental needs of everybody across all dimensions, not just for food, water and shelter, but also for education, health, economic security, voice, and purpose, amongst others. This is ethically important, economically efficient, and environmentally crucial (for example, birth rates decline dramatically once people's fundamental needs are met).

Secondly, it would live within planetary and local ecological limits and strengthen all life and ecosystems – sustainability is no longer enough, regeneration is critical.

Thirdly, it would maximise human wellbeing or flourishing and foster the development of empathy towards 'the other' – the stranger, the refugee.

Fourthly, it would greatly reduce inequalities both within and between countries.

Globally, we have more than sufficient resources and the necessary technologies to realise all the above goals.

To achieve these goals, it is crucial to learn from Nature. John Fullerton, an ex-banker, has developed principles for economy aligned with living system principles and the laws of physics. His landmark paper, *Regenerative Capitalism*,[147] is an articulation of what an economy aligned with living systems principles and the laws (not theories) of physics would look like. He points out that, according to leading evolutionary theorists,[148] there are patterns and principles that Nature (living and non-living alike) uses to build stable, healthy, and sustainable systems throughout the world.

Fullerton sets forth eight principles:

RIGHT RELATIONSHIPS: Holding the continuation of life as sacred and recognising that the human economy is embedded in human culture, which is itself embedded in the biosphere. All systems – from molecular all the way to cosmic – are nested, interconnected, and defined by over-arching win-win relationships of mutualism, within which the immediate exchanges take place.

INNOVATIVE, ADAPTIVE AND RESPONSIVE: Draws on the innate ability of human beings to innovate and 'create anew' across all sectors of society. Humans are innately creative and entrepreneurial. Even in failure, we begin again.

WEALTH IS VIEWED HOLISTICALLY: True wealth is not money in the bank. It is defined in terms of the wellbeing of the 'whole', achieved through the harmonisation of the multiple forms of capital, with systemic health only as strong as the weakest link. Wellbeing depends on belonging, on community, and on an array of community-stewarded assets.

PARTICIPATION IS EMPOWERED: All participants in a system must be empowered to participate in and contribute to the health of the whole. Therefore, beyond whatever moral beliefs one may hold, financial and non-financial wealth must be equitably (although not necessarily equally) distributed in the context of an expanded understanding of systemic health. As people, we long to be part of something bigger than ourselves.

ROBUST CIRCULATORY FLOW: Like the metabolism of any healthy system, resources (material and non-material) must circulate up and down the system efficiently and effectively. Circular economy concepts of material and energy are one important aspect of this principle at work in a regenerative economy.

'EDGE EFFECT' ABUNDANCE: Creative collaborations across sectors of the economy increase the possibility of value-adding wealth creation through a diversity of relationships, exchanges, and resiliency.

SEEKS BALANCE: Living within planetary boundaries, without collapse, requires economic systems that are designed for a balance of efficiency and resilience and are built on patterns and principles that mirror those found in resilient and healthy natural systems.

HONOURS COMMUNITY AND PLACE: Operating to nurture healthy, stable communities and regions, both real and virtual, in a connected mosaic of place-centred economies.[149]

Fullerton's principles are not absolutes. They are part of a rapidly emerging field of holistic thinking. These include what Kalle Lasn, in *Meme Wars*, refers to as:

> Social economists, feminist economists, interdisciplinary economists, behavioural economists, ecological economists and hundreds of intellectuals and maverick professors who

are openly critical of the neo-classical regime and are fighting to overthrow it.[150]

There are many examples, such as, ecological economics advocated by Herman Daly, winner of the Right Livelihood Award; human-scale development promoted by Manfred Max Neef, the Chilean economist, also winner of the Right Livelihood Award; the idea of Prosperity Without Growth, proposed by Tim Jackson; the work of the New Economics Foundation (NEF); those proposing Solidarity Economics, including the Fair Trade movement; the Cooperative movement, and the Transition Initiatives, including the Transition Town Movement, a grassroots community development project that promotes self-sufficiency with the aim to reduce economic instability, reliance on fossil fuels and the potentially destructive effect of human pursuit of wellbeing on the climate.

All these examples pose some common questions and challenges to humanity: they ask us to think again about value and wealth and the ways in which 'value in use' might differ from 'value in exchange' and, even more so, from 'value as a speculative commodity'.

They also ask us to think carefully about debt, making a distinction between the naturally wasting quality of the physical world and the apparently eternal and ever-growing world of debt, never wasting away, but ever growing by the mechanism of compound interest.

They further ask us to rethink the mantra of growth and its sibling, consumerism.

They point to the way in which, through the desire to measure with ever more minute accuracy, we have come to put quantity above quality and theory above experience. Thus, we are left with measures and theories that seem to be distant from the everyday.

They ultimately ask us to come to economics afresh with concerns that include economic justice, ecology, and community.

A good example is the Buen Vivir of the Andes, whose general principles of the good life are that there should be harmony and balance of all and with all, solidarity, complementarity, and equality, as well as collective wellbeing and the satisfaction of the basic needs of all in harmony with Mother Earth.[151] Also embedded in the project is the notion of Solidarity Economics:

> Solidarity economy designates all production, distribution and consumption activities that contribute to the democratisation of the economy based on citizen commitments both at a local and global level. It is carried out in various forms, in all continents. It covers different forms of organisation that the population uses to create its own means of work or to have access to qualitative goods and services, in a dynamic of reciprocity and solidarity which links individual interest to the collective interest. In this sense, solidarity economy is not a sector of the economy, but an overall approach that includes initiatives in most sectors of the economy.[152]

What is needed is a new type of economy that is open, dynamic, and entrepreneurial, while also being fair, locally rooted and where everybody feels valued. It needs to keep the best features of globalisation, while directly addressing globalisation's key problems. Is this combination achievable? Without question, it is! But it requires a radical shift in economic thinking and, above all, it requires basing our economies on a new set of values. At the heart of the new economy must be the same values and characteristics as those to which well-functioning families and households aspire. A survey in 2009 of 140,000 business people found that over two-thirds thought the economic crisis was also a values crisis and that they wished they could practise the same values at work as they do at home. This is what a new peaceful economy must make possible.

An economy based on the values of well-functioning families and households would be: rooted, fair, secure, flourishing, sustainable, welcoming, and creative. Let's expand on each of these:

ROOTED: People need to feel in control of their lives and this requires strong local democracy and strong local organisations. Energy and food need to be locally produced, wherever possible; local businesses need to be highly supported; rules need to be enacted to prevent undue competition from national and international businesses; banks should be dedicated to serving the local population; and cultural norms and customs must be allowed to flourish (provided they respect universal human rights and democratically agreed laws).

FAIR: This means not only a major reduction in inequality, but restoring trust in the major institutions of society: government, businesses, public bodies, media, banks, and non- governmental organisations. People have got to believe that these organisations are ethical and serving the public interest, rather than suspecting that the individuals within them are looking after their own interests at the expense of everybody else.

SECURE: It is going to be increasingly difficult for governments to ensure that there is full-time employment for everybody. One major factor will be new technological breakthroughs displacing traditional jobs. Just as universal education and health provision has been the norm for years in many rich countries, economic security for all throughout life needs to become a new norm. This would be a radical shift requiring exploring basic income provision, amongst other options. The cost of providing economic security for all would almost certainly require raising extra or new taxes, but would also inject new purchasing power into economies and greatly reduce the risk to people starting up small businesses or projects. It would also reduce the risks to people moving between jobs and facilitate businesses changing the size of their workforce.

FLOURISHING: Providing lifelong economic security will make people less vulnerable, but will not make them feel necessary. The norm must be that everybody contributes to society by doing something worthwhile and that this is recognised and valued, whether financially or otherwise. This would include effective nurturing of children, making useful products, providing needed services, artistic creation, improving the natural world, caring for others, and undertaking research (to name just a few areas). Encouraging and enabling everybody to contribute is the key to a flourishing society and economy. This principle is at the heart of stewardship and promoting the common good and addresses the deep wish of many humans to make a real difference in this world – however small!

SUSTAINABLE: The health and wellbeing of all of us, as well as other living things, depends on a healthy planet. Not only have we got to look after the planet much better, but we need to heal the harm we have already done. This requires a major focus on regeneration of the natural world.

WELCOMING: A locally-rooted economy can also be an open one. One where people feel valued and economically secure will be much more welcoming to people from other nations and it will be much less fearful about global trade and immigration. Knowledge transfer and international cooperation to tackle global issues can then become the norm.

CREATIVE: Enterprise, innovation and creativity would be valued, facilitated and rewarded in all areas. This will require not just healthy competition, but also collaboration and solidarity.

The peaceful economy will continue to be one based on a mixture of market and non-market activities, but it will operate according to the types of values set out above and with very different institutions. The institutional framework will include:

STRONG DEMOCRATIC ECONOMIC MANAGEMENT: This is required to determine which parts of the economy should be marketised and which not; to redistribute as necessary income, wealth, ownership and power; to manage markets effectively, including competition policies, incentives, and taxes and, where necessary, control of aggregate material inputs into market and waste outputs. It would also foster collaboration and solidarity in those sectors where this is more effective than fostering competition and vice versa. What is needed is smart and strategic governance – not big or small governments.

DIVERSITY AND APPROPRIATE SCALE: Diversity is critical for system resilience in most markets or areas of activity. We need private, public, and social enterprises; specialist and general organisations; large, medium and small banks; and local, regional, national, and international institutions. Appropriate scale means that an activity is usually best carried out at the smallest possible scale. Local production of food makes sense, whereas car or aircraft manufacture in each locality does not.

BUILDING BUSINESSES AND INSTITUTIONS WITH SOCIAL AND BIOCENTRIC DNA: The purpose of business needs to switch from that of making money to needing to make money to create real value for society. No longer can the creation of good jobs be only a cost and good environmental performance depend on regulation. Both need to be within the DNA of future businesses, together with the creation of great products and services and a fair return for investors.

REGENERATION AND EXTENSION OF THE GLOBAL COMMONS: Not only do the current global commons of the atmosphere, sea, polar regions, and the Earth's wild spaces need to be regenerated, but new commons need to be created, including capturing for the public benefit some of windfall gains of new technological breakthroughs.

PLACING LIMITS ON MATERIAL USAGE AND ECONOMIC GROWTH: In theory, if economic growth was totally decoupled from non-renewable resource usage and renewable resources were only used at their replacement rate, then economic growth could go on forever. In reality, this is not possible. Thus, economic growth will have to be limited for the richest nations and for the richest portion of people in these nations.

In any case, in the peaceful economy, economic growth ceases to be a goal. The goals of the economy are those set out earlier.

A NEW GLOBAL COMPACT: Not only will each nation have to plan to create long and flourishing lives for its citizens while living within its share of planetary limits, but the richer nations must collectively meet those costs of fundamental human need and regenerating planetary systems that poor nations cannot cover. This requires a new Global Marshall Plan.

An economy based on the above values and principles and with this type of institutional framework will be inherently far more peaceful than our current violent economy.

Firstly, it will halt and reverse the harm we are causing to our planet and all living creatures. This, in turn, will reduce the risk of human conflict over diminishing resources. Most importantly though, it will change our relationship with our planet and all other life. We will move from being masters and exploiters to caretakers and stewards, viewing the continuation of life as sacred and other life as our equals. This will bring harmony into our lives.

Building a much fairer and just economy will reverse the huge social harm caused by current inequalities. This will not only greatly improve the lives of those currently suffering, but it will boost the wellbeing of everybody. It will also embed the principle of justice into all aspects of our lives.

An economy that provides security and helps foster meaning in our lives will enable people to truly flourish. Such an economy will not only be far more peaceful, but also far more creative. Critically, it will radically alter how we view 'the other'. No longer do we have to be fearful of the other – the stranger, the immigrant – taking our jobs, our houses, or our culture. No longer will politicians have fertile ground in which to stoke populist nationalism.

Perhaps, above all, we will find peace because we will be living as our own true selves. We are not selfish individuals motivated primarily by wealth and success. We are related beings with a huge capacity to love. We urgently need an economic system that recognises this.

History shows that system change is possible if enough people want it and are prepared to work together to demand it. A majority of the population is not required to enable this – an organised minority is sufficient, provided they are telling a positive and compelling new story. I am cautiously optimistic because I believe the true story of who we are and the peaceful economy we desire has more potency than the false neoliberal story.

134.   Global Footprint Network: http://www.footprintnetwork.org/en/index.php/GFN/page/world_footprint/

135.   Oxfam, GB: https://www.oxfam.org/sites/www.oxfam.org/files/file_attachments/bp-economy-for-99-percent-160117-summ-en.pdf

136.   Edelman Trust Barometer: http://www.edelman.com/trust2017/

137.   World Population Prospects: Key findings and advanced tables, UN, 2015, https://esa.un.org/unpd/wpp/publications/files/key_findings_wpp_2015.pdf

138.   Jerome C Glenn, Elizabeth Florescu, 'Future Work/Technology 2050 Real-Time Delphi Study', 2015-2016, State of the Future Millennium Project, http://www.millennium-project.org/millennium/Future-WorkTechnology_2050.pdf

139.   Sebastian Junger, 2016, *Tribe: On Homecoming and Belonging*, Twelve.

140.   Aditya Chakrabortty, https://www.theguardian.com/commentisfree/2016/nov/22/just-about-managing-pontypool-south-wales-poverty-post-industrial-truth-britain,

141.   Manfred Max-Neef and Philip B Smith, 2011, *Economics Unmasked*, Dartington: Green Books.

142.   Steve Keen http://www.debtdeflation.com/blogs/2009/03/24/neoclassical-economics-mad-bad-and-dangerous-to-know/

143.   Ibid.

144.   Motesharrei, Safa, et al., 2014, 'Human And Nature Dynamical Study': HANDY, 'Modeling inequality and use of resources in the collapse or sustainability of societies', *Ecological Economics*, Volume 101, 90-102. http://www.sciencedirect.com/science/article/pii/S0921800914000615

145.   Ibid.

146.   Ibid.

147.   John Fullerton, 2015, 'Regenerative Capitalism', Capital Institute, http://capitalinstitute.

org/wp-content/uploads/2015/04/2015-Regenerative-Capitalism-4-20-15-final.pdf

148. Eric J Chaisson, 2002, *Cosmic Evolution, The Rise of Complexity in Nature*, Boston: Harvard University Press, http://www.hup.harvard.edu/catalog.php?isbn=9780674009875

149. Ibid.

150. Kalle Lasn, 2013, *Meme Wars,* Seven Stories Press.

151. See, for example, pachamama.org.

152. Edited by Jenna Allard, Carl Davidson and Julie Matthaei, 2008, *Solidarity Economy,* Chicago: ChangeMaker Publications, 6.

CHAPTER **TEN**

BEING BEFORE DOING: TRANSFORMATION THROUGH AN EDUCATION FOR PEACE

MARK A MILTON AND VICKI J MCCOY

WITH THE RECENT RISE IN authoritarian leadership and renewed efforts to suppress human freedoms in many countries around the world, it would be tempting to conclude that humanity is going backwards in time. The worldwide response in the last decades to the actions associated with authoritarianism, however, should give us hope. Events such as the 2002 'Peace from every balcony' rainbow flag campaign, protesting the impending war in Iraq, and the 2017 Women's March for human rights that involved an estimated five-million people on all seven continents are a confirmation of the truth that we as humans have evolved to a greater awareness of the intrinsic worth and potential of each human life. They are evidence of a collective deep and conscious desire for a more just and peaceful society in which each of us can fulfil our purpose.

Nowhere is this shift in human consciousness more apparent than among the new generation of youth, our future leaders. In working with young people, we at Education 4 Peace have been inspired by a growing number of them whose values are shaped by and manifested in their spiritual connectedness to one another and to Nature and whose desire is to create a world that is an accepting, good place for all to live. In this way, they are poised to realise the peaceful world we dream of. Our task now is to support them, to nurture the seeds of their potential to full flower by transforming our approach to education at this most promising moment in history.

This transformation is an education for emotional self-awareness and self-mastery that can help contribute to peaceful, nonviolent ways of being in the world, a transformation that is, in fact, already underway. Its foundation was laid by a shift in consciousness that began in the mid- to late-twentieth century, when psychology moved beyond the fields of science and medicine and into the mainstream of daily life. Indeed, the humanistic psychology movement of the 1950s kicked it off, taking a holistic and positive view of the human psyche, and our capacity for self-knowledge and personal growth. It was supported by the works of many, including American psychologists, Abraham Maslow, who proposed a hierarchy of shared human needs that motivate human behaviour, and Carl Rogers, who pioneered a person-centred approach to understanding ourselves and our relationships. In the 1980s and 1990s, the democratisation of psychology was significantly advanced with the emergence of the concept of emotional health. Work on emotional intelligence, positive psychology, and human resilience, as well as the development of nonviolent communication, all helped bring emotional health to the forefront of our consciousness.

Today, there is a widely-shared interest in emotional health, as evidenced by the number of books, workshops, and coaches dedicated to the subject. While its definition will vary across cultures and will certainly evolve with time, in general, emotional health can be understood as a state of emotional wellbeing that incorporates a growing consciousness of the impact of our emotions on the other aspects of our physical, mental, and spiritual health. Emotional health is a space that allows us to become aware of the quality of our presence, our mindsets and thoughts, and its impact on our life, relations, and environments. The French words *savoir*-être express it best — emotional health is, "knowing how to be", how to live with congruency between our deep values and our interactions with others and our environment. It is a space in which we become keen observers of our inner state of being, and we have the power of choice. With *savoir*-être, we are enabled to recognise that the lack of peace in the world outside may be a mirror reflection of the lack of peace within us as individuals. We can choose to let go of the activity and reactivity that often manifest in times of emotional upheaval, as we confront the inevitable frustrations, disappointments, and pain of human existence. In this way, we can begin to develop self-mastery, which is not about controlling or suppressing our emotions or thoughts. Rather it is about gaining so much experience in observing our emotions and thoughts that they no longer govern us, and, instead, we govern them. In short, emotional wellbeing is at the core of who we really are, a natural place of self-compassion, and it serves all life.

We are living in exciting times. We have entered a new millennium in self-awareness and our understanding of how to achieve emotional health. Now is the time for us to make the most of the wealth of such knowledge and wisdom and to act on it accordingly.

This, then, is the new role of education in the twenty-first century — to share with youth life-serving ways of being and to treat learning for emotional wellbeing as being equal in importance to subject knowledge and the other skills traditionally taught in schools. What is emerging now is a new spiritual consciousness for being and teaching which is transforming education. It is a model of the teacher as learner, coach, and mentor in helping to give birth to a peaceful, respectful society where individuals can fulfil their life's purpose in ways that benefit all of us collectively. It is a model of the classroom as an experiential space for learning and practising the tools and skills to help bring this world and society into being. That classroom may be in the home, on the football field, or in the school. Wherever its location, its purpose will be to foster in ourselves – the educators first, and then in the students – self-knowledge and a mastery of emotions that help foster greater self-esteem, self-responsibility, better relationships, less violence, and more meaningfulness in our life endeavours. In so doing, this transformative approach to education will transform our world.

This may sound naïve in the face of what is happening around us — the chaos, confusion, and violence we see in many parts of our world, even at times in our homes, schools, and playgrounds. However, we would do well to remind ourselves of the words of Buddhist teacher, Pema Chödrön, that, "The peace we are looking for is not peace that crumbles as soon as there is difficulty or chaos [...]" but, rather, "[...] an experience that's expansive enough to include all that arises without feeling threatened."[153]

BRINGING A PEACEFUL WORLD TO PASS: TRANSFORMING EDUCATION

The World Health Organization defines mental health as:

> A state of wellbeing in which every individual realizes his or her own potential, can cope with the normal stresses of life, can work productively and fruitfully, and is able to contribute to her or his community.[154]

The link between mental health and education is obvious: we seek to prepare youth to work and live successfully in the world, to achieve all that they desire and are capable of, and contribute to society. The link between emotional health and education, however, is pivotal and one we must develop and share with our youth, making it a routine part of their curriculum. It is emotional health that will allow youth to go beyond self-actualisation to the transcendent space of inner peace that will then be reflected in their interactions, connectedness, and contributions to the world outside.

What follows is an exploration of the key steps we may take if we desire to transform education in ways that will help bring a more peaceful world to pass.

THE TEACHER AS LEARNER AND COACH: As a new model for education emerges, being precedes doing. Those who aspire to teach must constantly ask, "Whom am I bringing to this encounter with the one I desire to teach?" This is not about harsh self-judgment, but rather an attitude based on a realisation that there are no hierarchies in self-awareness; rather there is a space that can be ever expanded. It is a shared learning journey of respectful giving and receiving that lasts a lifetime. The implications of this understanding are great, for as the psychologist and teacher, Haim Ginott, courageously stated:

> I've come to a frightening conclusion that I am the decisive element in the classroom. It's my personal approach that creates the climate. It's my daily mood that makes the weather. As a teacher, I possess a tremendous power to make a child's life miserable or joyous. I can be a tool of torture or an instrument of inspiration. I can humiliate or heal. In all situations, it is my response that decides whether a crisis will be escalated or de-escalated and a child humanized or dehumanized.[155]

The special challenge for us as adults is that, unlike the youth we teach or parent or coach, it is necessary for us to unlearn as well as learn. We need to unlearn old models of hierarchal teaching based on the, 'I give, you receive' transfer of knowledge from authority figure to student. We will then learn new ways to tame our own emotions, and model for those we teach effective ways to express feelings and needs. We will be called upon to demonstrate humility and be willing to say, "I don't know", rather than pretend to have all the answers. We will learn to listen closely to our students to hear the feelings and needs behind the words that are spoken and to offer life-enhancing approaches for how to get those needs met. We are in a transition phase from the old way to the new way of educating youth. It is a unique opportunity for all of us, and a shared adventure that allows us unlimited creativity for shaping the future of education.

CHOOSING SELF-RESPONSIBILITY: Instead of pouring into youth what we believe to be the knowledge they need to survive in this world, we are empowering youth to become evolved human beings, capable of self-responsibility, i.e., knowing themselves and what they need, and able to find effective strategies to meet their needs in ways that enhance all life.

For example, through education, we can help youth to understand the difference between being a victim and choosing a victim mindset that externalises responsibility for our emotions and wellbeing. As demonstrated by the 27 years South African leader, Nelson Mandela, spent in prison for opposing apartheid and the three years Austrian Holocaust survivor, Viktor Frankl, spent in Nazi concentration camps, victimisation can and does occur in human life, often without our consent and against our will. Just so, on another scale of victimisation, a young person could be a victim of an unjust decision by an authority figure, or a bully on the playground. What we learn from the examples of President Mandela and Dr Frankl, however, is instructive for all of us in every area of life at any age: both men made the conscious choice to take self-responsibility for their thoughts, emotions, and behaviours while in circumstances outside their control. That is what made all the difference in the quality of their lives and allowed them to go on to contribute to the betterment of humankind. Dr Frankl put it eloquently when he wrote:

> Everything can be taken from a man but one thing: the last of human freedoms – to choose one's attitude in any given set of circumstances, to choose one's own way.[156]

The new education we offer youth can help them to recognise this freedom of choice in attitude in all circumstances, an irrevocable power that resides in each of us. It can support them in finding their own way through awareness of their feelings and needs, empowering them to deal effectively with the adversity that is part of every human life. It can offer them the opportunity to experience the freedom of self-responsibility for their thoughts, emotions, and actions, even as they stand up for their values.

LISTENING WITH ALL OF OUR BEING: One of the keys to awareness and mastery of our emotions that is available to all might be described as *learning to listen and listening to learn*. When we are in our mother's womb, the first sense that develops is our hearing. In utero, we listen to our mother's heartbeat and take comfort from it. Out in the world, we discover that there is listening that goes beyond what we hear with our ears — a listening with our whole body, with our mind, our heart and all of our senses. As the poet, philosopher and psychotherapist, Gary L Whited, explains:

> Though we think of listening most often as the experience of sound landing in our auditory capacity to hear, at its essence listening is receptivity, and we receive in many ways. [...] It can be our ears we offer to the words someone speaks, so we hear their story. It can be the heart we offer to the outpouring of another's grief as we hear of their loss. It can be the hand we offer to someone's reach for help, our mind that receives the imprint of another's idea, or the entire body that receives the invitation of a lover.[157]

One form of our all-body capacity for listening is 'empathetic listening', as described by American psychologist, Marshall B Rosenberg, in his ground-breaking book, *Nonviolent Communication: A Language of Life*. As teachers, parents and coaches, we often listen intellectually, with opinions, points of view, and judgments, either positive or negative, that enable us to diagnose, assess, advise and critique. We are formulating our response, even as the student or youth is speaking. In empathetic listening, we recognise the truth in Dr Rosenberg's assertion that, "Every message, regardless of form or content, is an expression of a need," – and we follow his advice that, "Our goal is to create a quality of empathic connection that allows everyone's needs to be met."[158]

The needs of which he speaks can be distinguished from the strategies we use to meet needs. Needs are common to all of us and they exist within us, even if we acquiesce to their suppression. Rosenberg identifies many needs – including the need for autonomy, celebration, integrity, interdependence, play, spiritual communion, and physical nurturance, in all their many forms – as needs we share. There is no conflict that occurs between us over the needs themselves; our needs are internal to each of us. The conflict in human relationships occurs over the externalised strategies we use to meet our needs.

The quickest way to connect to our needs is to pay attention to the emotions we have when our needs are fulfilled or not fulfilled. If we are feeling angry, for example, we may discover that our need for respect has not been met. If we feel joyous, we may find that our need for appreciation has been fulfilled. This is the power of our empathetic connection to ourselves and to others. It allows us to seek fulfilment of our own needs, while respecting and honouring the needs of others.

When teachers, parents or coaches are able to listen to themselves, observing their own feelings and the needs that create them, and can respond with self-compassion rather than self-judgment, they are more prepared to listen empathetically to their children or students. It goes without saying that empathetic listening will be most successfully taught when it is also being modelled by the one who seeks to teach it.

One of the common challenges to empathetic listening is our addiction to distractions and our discomfort with silence. Through simple practices such as listening to a partner for five minutes with complete attention, without interrupting or commenting, we experience the power of silence in listening. As listeners, we find ourselves able to connect beyond the rational content to what the speaker is living, his or her feelings and needs, without validating, comparing or judging. Often, speakers in such exchanges find themselves heard in a way that is deeply satisfying, and listeners find offering this experience to be a privilege. As we learn to observe our own listening behaviours and comfort levels, we open up the power of choice in how we relate to ourselves and to one another. Empathetic listening enhances our human connection and helps to create peace.

TAMING SILENCE: Silence is the entry door to listening. In learning and teaching empathetic listening, both teacher and student can come to recognise the difference between empty silence and full silence. In empty silence, one or both parties are uncomfortable with silence. In full silence, rich communication occurs, and we may even connect to others at a deep level that is beyond words. A simple way to experience the power of full silence is to make direct eye contact with someone who is providing a service for you, for example, handing you food at a café. Convey with your eyes that you truly see the person. The few words you speak, such as, "Thank you," will simply validate a life-affirming connection that has already occurred in the silence.

Most of us are uncomfortable with silence. If we start to welcome the discomfort of silence, we can start to discover what's behind the discomfort. It can be very different from one person to the next, but usually it has to do with emptiness, or questions that start to arise that we are uncomfortable with. Learning to be open, to become comfortable with the space of not knowing, and not trying to understand is the beginning of a new journey. We suddenly enter a new space where we begin to actually experience the events of life differently because we are not trying unconsciously to fill up space, sound, and time.

With patience, becoming familiar with silence is something we can learn for ourselves and teach youth as part of their educational curriculum. Taming silence has the power to radically enhance the quality of all of our lives. For as the fox says to the boy in Antoine de Saint-Exupéry's *The Little Prince*, "If you want a friend, tame me."[159]

THE POWER OF OBSERVATION: Another of the great gifts of conscious listening is our heightened awareness of our own interiority. In preparation for deep listening, we learn to ask ourselves, "What space am I in? Am I with myself or am I with you?" If I am with you, I may ask myself, "Am I in an intellectual space where I seek rational understanding and I have opinions? Or am I in touch with what is alive within me and you, état-*d'être*, connecting to my own and your emotions, needs, and values?" When we can become observers of what it is we are feeling and the space we are in, new possibilities and choices open up for us. Observation is itself a form of listening.

There are two forms or places of observation of our needs and feelings: one, when we are in a specific situation, especially one that is uncomfortable; and, secondly, when the situation has passed. In the first space, when we are living an uncomfortable moment, we actually have the choice either to put our energy into trying to get out of it – which sometimes is necessary – or to acknowledge and accept it, and to experience what happens while we stay in that state of being. The thirteenth century Persian poet, scholar and Sufi mystic, Jalāl Al-Dīn Rūmī, advocated grateful acceptance of such discomfort in his famous poem, *The Guest House*:

> This being human is a guest house.
> Every morning a new arrival.
> A joy, a depression, a meanness,
> some momentary awareness comes
> As an unexpected visitor.
> Welcome and entertain them all!
> Even if they're a crowd of sorrows,
> who violently sweep your house
> empty of its furniture,
> still treat each guest honorably.
> He may be clearing you out
> for some new delight.
> The dark thought, the shame, the malice,
> meet them at the door laughing,
> and invite them in.
> Be grateful for whoever comes,
> because each has been sent
> as a guide from beyond.[160]

Rumi understood the learning potential of this space of discomfort. If we accept it, we are transforming our future capacity for observation, without even consciously realising it. When we get out of this space of discomfort, which we all eventually do, the learning is very different than it would be if we had tried to get out of it. The psychotherapist and teacher, John Welwood, known for his pioneering work in integrating psychological and spiritual work, suggests that the only way we can free ourselves from conditioned patterns of behaviour is to have a full, conscious experience of them, rather than running away from them.

The freedom of which Dr Welwood speaks is an outcome of being able to observe, stay with, and process our feelings, no matter how painful they are in the moment. While the learning comes after the experience, rather than during it, the learning is very powerful because we have increased our resilience and our space for observation relative to what happened, as well as in terms of what may happen in the future. We are able to see the past experience for what it really was, with a certain detachment that doesn't hang on emotions or beliefs. Our increased capacity for self-witness enhances our freedom to make choices when we go into difficult moments in the future.

Observation, in effect, creates a space of freedom and creativity in which we can choose to create our own experiences. We are no longer in victim-thinking, attached to the idea that other people or events hold the key to our inner state. We are self-responsible, aware of our feelings and needs/values and of our inner power of choice regarding intention, attitude, and action.

Just as there are many pathways to self-awareness, there are also many pathways to self-observing. One that is proving to be highly successful is Dr Richard C Schwartz's Internal Family Systems Model, often referred to as self-leadership. This non-pathologising approach to self-observation recognises the multiplicity of the mind, with its many sub-parts that often have conflicting agendas. We experience this conflict in situations in which we have a hesitation or a doubt, and a part of us thinks one way and another part thinks a different way. Creating peace among these sub-parts can be achieved by acknowledging and exploring their needs and protective intentions; and by inviting the Self, our calm, centred, and unconflicted true nature at the core of our being, to lead us. Self-leadership is a practice that is accessible to all people beyond the realm of psychotherapy and, as such, holds great promise for application in the new education of youth.

Through observation of the different parts of our being, we enter a space of autonomy and conscious awareness of interdependence. We recognise that the causes are inside each of us and that we then have as many solutions as we can create. We have discernment and can ask ourselves, "Is the part that is leading getting me where I want to go?" Becoming a true observer means we are in greater mastery of our emotions and thoughts. When we learn to observe with awareness, it transforms our reality. This is a skill we want to make available to our youth as part of their education. They can only learn it by experiencing it.

TRANSFORMATION THROUGH EDUCATION: TWO STORIES

In 1976, the French physician, writer and philosopher, Henri Laborit, said that the daily lives of people will be transformed when societies are as concerned with conveying, even to their youth, as much information about who they are and what 'makes them tick' rather than just teaching them how to produce economically. The transformation of which he spoke, more than four decades ago, is now underway through social and emotional learning — including mindfulness, identifying and naming emotions, and listening to others to better manage frustrations and conflicts. Individuals and organisations have made it their mission over the last two decades to bring this learning to the new generation. The following are two examples of many that are happening across the world.

EDUCATION 4 PEACE

Reflecting on our own experience, the Swiss-based foundation, Education 4 Peace (E4P), has been advocating for and supporting emotional health programmes in the fields of education and sports since 2002. In 2007, E4P initiated with its partner, the International Federation of Telephone Emergency Services, the first International Congress on Emotional Health, co-sponsored by the World Health Organization.

E4P's collaboration with national and international football associations to teach the skills required to master our emotions are an example of the potential that exists to make this learning a part of tomorrow's education on a broader scale. Peter Gillieron, Chairman of the Union of European Football Associations' Fair Play and Social Responsibility Committee, asserts that the game of football is our society in microcosm. He points out that, in football, as in life, there are tensions, emotions, and violence, as well as examples of teamwork, solidarity, and friendship. E4P has found that sports provide boundless opportunities for teaching and learning about self-awareness and fostering empathy to improve behaviours in relating to others and in handling adversity and setbacks. All the emotions of life are there, but experienced in rapid succession and compressed into a few hours: elation over a goal, frustration when the referee throws a red card, anger when one player fouls another, joy when a match is won, disappointment when a match is lost. Competition ramps up the intensity of these emotions, opening the door for violence, or other inappropriate behaviour.

What E4P has discovered can be applied in many other settings: that we can learn the skills of self-awareness and emotional mastery in the same way that football players can learn to master the ball — with practise. In educating thousands of coaches, referees, and players on how to practise the empathetic listening and observation skills that can lead to healthy competition and prevent violence on the sports field, E4P has identified attitude as the fifth skill, along with technique, tactics, fitness, and mind, that are all needed to excel in this game and in life. Emotions impact our energy levels, our concentration, and our motivation, on and off the field. Learning to master our emotions improves the quality of our lives, our happiness, our wellbeing, and our capacity for contribution. These are skills we want our youth to have from their earliest days, and focused education offers that possibility.

A competitive environment, such as that found on the sports field and in many business enterprises and schools today, poses real challenges to teaching these important life skills that lead to inner and outer peace. If competition becomes a goal in itself and winning is all that matters, then education is undermined. On the other hand, when competition is a way of exploring our abilities, of learning and challenging ourselves to new heights, and when it's done with respect for ourselves and others, then competition can lead to greater self-awareness and self-mastery, to behaviours that serve life. The great virtue of competition is that it is a practice field for meeting adversity in any area of our lives. With self-awareness, we can ask ourselves, "What is my intention when I am in competition? What is my intention toward my opponent? Do I desire to win at any cost? Or do I want to do and be my best while respecting my opponent?" When we are consciously aware of our intention toward our opponent and can bring the benevolence and compassion that lie within us to bear on the playing field, we grow our capacity to respond effectively to any adversity.

GUADALUPE ALTERNATIVE PROGRAMS

For the non-profit Guadalupe Alternative Programs (GAP) in Minnesota, United States, the Internal Family System's self-leadership model has become an important part of their service delivery to communities challenged by poverty and, more recently, growing refugee populations. GAP is best known for providing educational and enrichment opportunities, training, and social and emotional support in 'alternative schools' for youth with emotional and behavioural problems, or related circumstances that keep them from attending regular public schools.

Linking their work to existing state priorities for addressing social and emotional learning, GAP's associate director and a licensed therapist, Dr Jody Nelson, and her colleagues have introduced thousands of students and teachers to the principles and practice of self-leadership. Youth learn how to distinguish their polarised parts, for example, a part that reacts with anger in adversity and another part that is sad at the consequences of lashing out in anger. They learn to have compassion for their parts, rather than shaming or rejecting them. They learn how to access Self at the calm centre of their being, allowing it to serve as a mediator between and among polarised parts, and a leader in choosing peaceful solutions to life's challenges. GAP schools have innovated the Connecting Room, a space where young people who are not feeling connected to themselves and others can go, or be sent by a teacher. In this space, 'all parts are welcome'. There is no judgment or punishment, but rather supportive school staff members prepared to help students sort out their parts so that they can return to class.

In the twelve years of offering self-leadership training in public, alternative, and charter schools, GAP has discovered core truths that apply to all schools that seek to incorporate the mastery of emotions and self-responsibility into educational curriculums. The first is that those who wish to teach self-leadership must begin by getting in touch with their own parts that are triggered by the behaviour of students. Some teachers are faced with unlearning patterns of behaviour in which their 'manager' part takes over in trying circumstances, and learning to allow their compassionate Self to take the lead. The second truth is that school environments must also be addressed as they are systems with 'parts' that traditionally rely on a control/submission model, rather than the compassion and empathy that support a new education for peace.

FROM THE VICIOUS CYCLE TO THE VIRTUOUS CYCLE

The transformation of education that is underway provides the understanding and tools for breaking the vicious cycle of how we respond to life's adversities. It does so by replacing it with a virtuous cycle that leads to peace. In this new education, we learn that if we respond to violence with violence, even in just criticising what we don't want, we remain in the energy of the vicious cycle. While it is necessary to have the courage to renounce violence and other attitudes that generate suffering, this alone is only a first step and will not bring about the peaceful human relationships and society we seek. What transforms our world is when we activate the virtuous cycle, moment by moment, adversity after adversity. We do this when we respect our own and others' feelings and values; when we practise empathy and non-judgment towards ourselves and others; when we listen deeply and communicate without blaming and criticising; when we take self-responsibility for our wellbeing; and when we observe and purify our intention towards our adversaries, so that we can remain in relationship, even when we disagree. This is the greatest gift we can offer the next generation: an education that lights the pathway to the virtuous cycle and supports all of us in being the peace we want to see in the world.

153. P Chödrön and S Boucher, 2012, *Taking The Leap*, Boston: Shambhala.

154. http://www.who.int/features/factfiles/mental_health/en/

155. H G Ginott, 1972, *Teacher and Child: A Book for Parents and Teachers*, New York: Collier-Macmillan.

156. V E Frankl, 1984, *Man's Search for Meaning: An Introduction to Logotherapy*, New York: Simon & Schuster.

157. G L Whited, 2015, 'Listening to our Listening', *The Wayfarer: A Journal of Contemplative Literature*, Spring.

158. M B Rosenberg, 2003, *Nonviolent Communication: A Language of Life*, CA: PuddleDancer Press.

159. A D Saint-Exupéry and K Woods, 1943, *The Little Prince*, New York: Harcourt, Brace & World.

160. Jalāl Al-Dīn Rūmi, Translated by C Barks, 1997, *The Essential Rumi*.

EPILOGUE

DRAWING ON OUR ONGOING EXPERIENCE with the work of the Spirit of Humanity Forum, and, in particular, the conversations from the series of dialogues on Peacefulness organised by the Guerrand-Hermès Foundation for Peace, in partnership with the Fetzer Institute and Reykjavik Peace Centre, this book has set out to develop the narrative of Peacefulness. Of course, in these proceeding pages, we have barely begun to tell that story and we are aware of how much more there is to discover and explore. Nevertheless, it has become clear to us that a critical part of this story is the manner in which we join personal aspirations and experiences of peacefulness within our lives, within local communities and with politics, work and action in the world.

The questions that we invited our contributors to investigate through this current project were centred around an understanding of what Peacefulness is, the necessary socio-economic and political conditions that would enable our peacefulness to flourish, and the kind of educative processes that would nurture human peacefulness. What then have we learned?

The most significant insight emerging from the book is that Peacefulness arises from our innate being, with its source in spirituality. Being peaceful is the condition that enables us to bring our spiritual ways of being into the wider realms of the world in such a manner that there is no such division between the inner and outer life. Instead, this book has shown that the inner-outer is a continuum, an integral process.

Equally significant is the idea that peace resides in the right relationships amongst all that is, including not only our relationships with each other, and between nations, but also, most importantly, the interdependence between the human world and other beings on our planet. From this, we have learned that relational peace is not simply given through external conditioning, it relies on our collective intention and mutual aspiration to cocreate a culture of peace together.

This takes us to the next point that peace does not necessarily rule out the conflictual nature of relationship. Therefore, in designing socio-economic systems and political and institutional structures, processes and steps must be put in place so that contemplation, dialogue, listening, and narrative sharing can be prioritised in our cultures and practices to help transform conflict into creative impetus.

Furthermore, we also learned that the forms of economy and society aimed at fostering Peacefulness must be those emphasising the wholeness of our being, common goods, and the deeply entangled and mutually supporting relationships that lie therein.

As for education, it has become clear that education is not preparation for our society's workforce, nor is it the process of reproducing and imposing disciplines and orders. Rather, education is itself a site for nurturing Peacefulness by co-constructing schools as communities, enriching the myriad relationships within the learning environment, and by cultivating holistic wellbeing in both teachers and students.

We hope that these small steps will become part of a much longer and increasingly well-travelled pathway towards what we see as an urgent and necessary evolution.

BIOGRAPHIES OF CONTRIBUTORS

FOUR ARROWS (WAHINKPE TOPA) AKA DON TRENT JACOBS is a Professor of Leadership Studies at the Fielding Graduate University. Formerly Dean of Education at Oglala Lakota College and tenured Associate Professor at Northern Arizona University, he has authored 21 books relating to wellness, critical theory, education, and the Indigenous worldview. The Alternative Education Resource Organisation (AERO) elected him as one of 27 visionaries for their text, and he is the recipient of a number of recognitions for his activism, including the Martin-Springer Institute's Moral Courage Award.

DAVID CADMAN is a Harmony Professor of Practice at the University of Wales Trinity St David (UWTSD), a Visiting Professor at the University of Maryland, an Associate of the Guerrand-Hermès Foundation for Peace and a consultant to the Fetzer Institute, Michigan, USA. He is also the Coordinator of the Harmony Project, a collaboration between the UWTSD and the Sustainable Food Trust. He has worked extensively with the Spirit of Humanity Forum. His latest publications are *Finding Elsewhere* (Zig Publishing, 2015) and, as co-editor, *Why Love Matters* (Peter Lang, 2016).

SCHERTO R. GILL is a Senior Research Fellow at the Guerrand-Hermès Foundation for Peace and Visiting Fellow at the University of Sussex, UK. She writes in the fields of education, peace and dialogue. Her most recent publications include *Redefining Religious Education: Spirituality and Human Flourishing* (Palgrave, 2013), *Critical Narrative as Pedagogy* (Bloomsbury, 2014), *Education as Humanisation* (Routledge, 2016), *Human-Centered Education* (Routledge, 2017), *Understanding Peace Holistically* (Peter Lang 2018). Scherto is a Fellow of the RSA, Associate of the Taos Institute, Board Member of the Spirit of Humanity Forum, Board Member of the Ara Pacis Initiative, and Trustee of Lewes New School, UK.

MAUREEN GOODMAN has been Programme Coordinator at the International Centre of the Brahma Kumaris World Spiritual University in London for the past seven years. She has worked with a variety of community groups, developing the university's outreach work in prisons, healthcare, education, women's issues, and interfaith dialogue. She is part of the European coordinating team for the Living Values Educational Initiative. She was UK national coordinator for the largest non-fundraising project for the

United Nations International Year of Peace (1986), The Million Minutes of Peace, and for the follow-on project, Global Co-operation for a Better World (1998-91).

STEVE KILLELEA is an accomplished entrepreneur and a renowned philanthropist. In 2000, he established The Charitable Foundation (TCF), one of the largest private overseas aid organisations in Australia, which specialises in working with the poorest communities of the world. The number of direct beneficiaries is estimated at 2.6 million people. In 2007, he founded the Institute for Economics and Peace (IEP), whose groundbreaking research includes the Global Peace Index, the world's leading measure of peacefulness. He currently serves on a number of influential company boards, advisory boards, and president councils. He has also received numerous awards, including the Order of Australia and the Luxembourg Peace Prize for his service to the global peace movement and the provision of humanitarian aid to the developing world.

MARIANNE MARSTRAND is the Executive Director of the Global Peace Initiative of Women (GPIW), an international NGO under the stewardship of women spiritual leaders. Over the past 15 years, she has helped organise many gatherings around the world on peacebuilding, youth leadership, ecology, compassionate economics, and the sacred feminine – themes that are close to her heart. Prior to her work with GPIW, she served as Project Coordinator for Karma Thegsum Tashi Gomang in Crestone, Colorado under the auspices of His Highness, the Gyalwa Karmapa. She deeply believes that the world needs the feminine wisdom to reawaken to our interconnectedness and the honouring of the sacredness of the Earth and reverence for all of life. Marianne resides in New York City and is a student of Sufi mystic, Llewellyn Vaughan-Lee. www.gpiw.org

VICKI J. MCCOY is an organisational development and communications consultant and the president of McCoy Communications & Training, LLC, in Atlanta, Georgia, USA. She has an insider's perspective on the functioning of government from her early career leading communications programmes in three US government agencies. As a press officer during the Panama Canal Treaty negotiations, she realised that the development of self-aware organisations and individuals was key to effective communication and the peaceful settlement of disputes. This led her to personally explore the subjects of self-awareness and team-building and to attain the qualifications to help others. She is the cocreator of a comprehensive development programme called 'Raising the Bar: Empowering Greatness in Individuals and Teams' and a registered neutral (mediator) in the State of Georgia. She was born in the United States, but raised in the Republic of Panama.

JOSEPH MILNE was an Honorary Lecturer at the University of Kent. His interests range from Platonism to medieval mysticism and theology. He is also interested in the tradition of scriptural exegesis from Origen to Hugh of St Victor and Meister Eckhart. His current research is into the classical and medieval understanding of Natural Law. He is Editor of *Land & Liberty*, the journal of the Henry George Foundation of Great Britain. He is author of the Temenos Academy papers, *The Ground of Being: Foundations of Christian Mysticism* (2004), *Metaphysics and the Cosmic Order* (2008), and *The Mystical Cosmos* (2013). He is a Trustee of The Eckhart Society and a Fellow of the Temenos Academy.

MARK MILTON is the Founder and Director of the Swiss-based foundation, Education 4 Peace (E4P). Created in 2002, the Foundation works internationally to promote the incorporation of skills in self-awareness, deep listening, and the mastery of emotions into the educational curriculum of youth, including sports education. From 2001-2010, he was Chairman of the International Federation of Telephone Emergency Services, with 600 centres in 28 countries. He initiated many activities to promote listening skills, as well as the first International Congress on the theme of Emotional Health in 2007, cosponsored by the World Health Organization. He has led E4P's ground-breaking work with international football federations to officially introduce self-awareness and teach skills in deep listening and empathetic communication that pave the way for nonviolent problem solving. He is the coauthor of *Football: A Path to Self-Awareness*.

GARRETT THOMSON is the Compton Professor of Philosophy at the College of Wooster, USA. He received his Ph.D. from the Oxford University. He is also the Chief Executive Officer of the Guerrand-Hermès Foundation for Peace. He is the author of numerous books including, *Needs, Thales to*

Sextus and *Bacon to Kant.* He coedited the six-volume *The Longman Standard History of Philosophy.* He is the coauthor/editor with Scherto Gill of *Human-Centred Education* (Routledge, 2017) and *Redefining Religious Education: Spirituality and Human Flourishing.* He was the CEO of the World Subud Association in 2005-2010.

STEWART WALLIS was Executive Director of the New Economics Foundation (NEF) until 2016. NEF is the UK's leading think tank in promoting social, economic, and environmental justice. A graduate of Cambridge and London Business School, his career has spanned from the World Bank to Oxfam, for which work he was awarded an OBE. He is on the Board of the New Economy Coalition (NEC) in the USA and he is a Fellow of the Club of Rome, a Steward of the World Economic Forum's Inclusive Growth Global Challenge, and a member of the Global Future Council on Values and Technology. He is working closely with the new Institute for Social Futures at Lancaster University and was awarded an Honorary Doctorate by the university.

INDEX

G

H

22271073R00137

Printed in Poland
by Amazon Fulfillment
Poland Sp. z o.o., Wrocław